Thinking
Out of the
Box

Thinking
Out of the
Box

---

*How to Market Your Company
into the Future*

Kathy C. Yohalem

John Wiley & Sons, Inc.

New York • Chichester • Weinheim • Brisbane • Singapore • Toronto

To the happy memory of my father who always encouraged me to "try everything" and "go for it."

And to Bea and Hunter and Bea and Norman for always being there for me.

Library of Congress Cataloging-in-Publication Data:

Yohalem, Kathy.
    Thinking out of the box : how to market your company into the future / by Kathy Yohalem.
      p.   cm.
    Includes index.
    ISBN 0-471-13916-5 (cloth : alk. paper)
    1. Marketing—Decision making. 2. Marketing—Management.
3. Strategic planning. I. Title. II. Title: How to market your company into the future.
HF5415.135.Y64   1997
658.8'02—DC20   96-34863

Printed in the United States of America

10 9 8 7 6 5 4 3 2 1

Acknowledgments

To Diane Specht, president of Word Services, for her invaluable help in making me better understand the difference between writing and speaking, helping to put the ideas and concepts into writing, and for her professional excellence in helping shape the editorial content.

To Ruth Mills, Editor, John Wiley & Sons, Inc., for her professionalism, many excellent suggestions, and helping me understand the literary process.

To the influencers and mentors in my career, Manny Kay, Stanford Makover, Jim Egan, and Sy Jones.

To my dear friends and colleagues who always encourage me to "just do it."

Contents

PART III   THINKING OUT OF THE BOX: LET'S GET SPECIFIC   145

How do you implement a Strategic Marketing Plan that actuates your corporate vision and creates added value? Use tactics that accentuate the positive and eliminate the negative in 5 critical business areas: infrastructure, marketing, human resources, technology, and logistics.

DOES BRAND EQUITY DRIVE
PART IV **YOUR BUSINESS?** 177

*Yes, you can also use "thinking out of the box" to
protect your brand equity—and cash in on it, too.*

PART V CYBERTRAKS 205

*Cybertraks—vital demographic, social, and
technological trends—offer opportunities for
growth as you move into the next millennium. It's
an exciting, new world if you know where you are
going.*

APPENDIX 253

Exhibits

Introduction

Take the lead in the introduction of a new order of things.

Machiavelli, *The Prince*, 1532

Your company is moving rapidly into a demanding future controlled by emerging technologies, global communications, and unrelenting competition. In this business climate, finding appropriate solutions to issues is critical; yet too often just defining the problems can be overwhelming.

Where can you turn? Whether you are the CEO of an old line corporation or an entrepreneur with a fledgling business, whether your company resides on Fashion Avenue or in Silicon Valley, whether you market soap to consumers or gaskets to industrial concerns or operate a maintenance service, the principles and techniques of strategic marketing can provide the answers you need to assure your company's continuing survival.

So what is *strategic* marketing? Like most business owners and executives, you may still think of marketing as a collection of sales support functions including public relations, advertising, and promotion. But marketing has evolved into a discipline that embraces every aspect of your company. When implemented properly, "the new marketing" gives you the tools to systematically move your company into the next millennium.

Thinking Out of the Box is a practical, informative, and entertaining guide to putting strategic marketing to work for your business today. Written in plain and simple language, it is a quick easy read that doesn't require a Ph.D. Any executive, middle manager, or person in business can benefit from this fast-paced book. *Thinking Out of the Box* demonstrates how, step by step.

- How can you create a company vision without being a visionary?
- How can a strategic plan market your company into the future?
- How can you finally feel in control of your company's destiny?
- What critical role does the consumer play in your corporate planning?
- What is the Strategic Value Chain? How does it affect your unique competitive advantage?
- How can you involve your colleagues in a team approach to implementing a strategic marketing plan?

Thinking Out of the Box answers these and many other questions. It shows you how to begin thinking creatively using the LINKS (Leverage Ideas to Navigate Key Strategies) method. It explains why the New Consumerism must be at the heart of every decision you make. And *Thinking Out of the Box* tells you how you can survive and prosper in the 21st century.

PART I

CREATING THE VISION

1

Are You Ready for the Twenty-First Century?

The human mind, once stretched to a new idea, never goes back to its original dimensions.

Oliver Wendell Holmes, American physician,
professor, and writer

As we move toward the 21st century, the ability to understand and apply the techniques of strategic marketing has become essential to a company's continuing survival. Yet most business owners and corporate executives know too little about the principles of strategic marketing and planning. They still see marketing as a collection of sales support functions, such as public relations, advertising, and promotion. Perhaps that's the extent of the marketing role in your company. Even if that is only partially true, be prepared to change the way you think about this and every other aspect of your company. That's a big order. How do you start?

Has your neighbor, friend, or spouse ever made a brilliant observation about your business? Perhaps your best friend made an offhand suggestion that startled you with its clarity of thought. Chances are your friend isn't a marketing genius.

Exhibit 1–1
In the Box

He simply isn't boxed in by the chiseled-in-granite attitudes that weigh down most companies like the man in Exhibit 1–1.

He doesn't know that selling direct to customers, for example, would upset your distribution system. He doesn't understand that a new product wouldn't fit into your manufacturing and distribution capabilities. Or he doesn't understand that your accounting service has no previous experience with industrial clients. And he doesn't realize you don't want to do *anything* that would disrupt a particular area of your company that is running smoothly. Since no one ever told him, "We don't do it that way," he is free to come up with his innovative idea.

Of course, your best friend doesn't have the answer to your company's problems. The idea of the naive outsider who blows away the cobwebs and transforms a stodgy company overnight may play in the movies, but it's a formula for disaster in real life. Thorough, firsthand knowledge of a company and its customers is absolutely essential to the development of a strategic marketing plan. The secret is to take the shackles off your mind and use that knowledge constructively as a springboard for finding new solutions to your company's issues.

It isn't easy. We are, unfortunately, creatures of habit. We make our choices and stick with them until they become deeply ingrained. Relying on habit weakens our ability to think creatively. Like a computer with too little RAM, brains become sluggish. The unexercised mind keeps returning to the same easy solutions even when those solutions no longer work.

For example, assume you must drive from point A to point B every day. In the beginning, you will probably choose the shortest, most direct route. That route soon becomes a habit. But what do you do if the road deteriorates or the neighborhood becomes dangerous? What if everyone else is going in the same direction and traffic becomes congested? How long do you wait before finding another way to reach your destination? And what opportunities are you missing by not exploring other routes? Maybe it's even time to rethink your destination or your point of origin. When habit rules your life, those thoughts never have a chance to surface.

■ **Thinking Out of the Box**

How do you break away from habit and start thinking creatively? Just as the body needs exercise, so does the mind. Let's start with a *mind-stretcher* that I call *Thinking Out of the Box*. It's an exercise with a few easy solutions and many tough ones. You will need paper, pencil, and at least ten uninterrupted minutes.

Draw a square and divide it into four areas of *equal* size and shape. Easy? Okay, draw another square and find an alternative way to divide it into four equal parts. Find as many alternative solutions as you can. It isn't easy, so take your time. And don't turn the page until you have found as many solutions as possible.

Exhibit 1–2
Easy Solution One

Exhibit 1–3
Easy Solution Two

Exhibit 1–4
Stretching the Box

How many did you draw? Two? Three? How many ways do you think it can be done? Chances are your first solution looks like Exhibit 1–2—two straight lines, one drawn horizontally, the other vertically. Like the straight line between point A and point B, it's fast, it's obvious, and it does the job. Does your second box look like Exhibit 1–3—diagonal lines cutting from corner to corner? This too is relatively obvious. Both solutions are almost reflex actions—just as most responses to situations that arise in business are reflexes.

Thinking beyond the easy solutions requires effort and originality. In Exhibit 1–4, three straight lines dividing the box into four rectangles, is more of stretch, but it leads to many variations. Look at Exhibit 1–5. Like Exhibit 1–3, each divides the square in half, then divides the two halves into two equal parts. The permutations are endless.

The boxes in Exhibit 1–6 have been modified with the addition of right angles. This modification offers a springboard for infinite variants. No one said you had to draw straight lines! The curved, pinwheel shape can be the basis for unlimited alternatives.

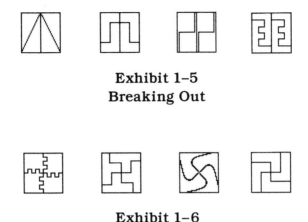

Exhibit 1–5
Breaking Out

Exhibit 1–6
Infinite Solutions

The Top Line

When we stop drawing straight lines from point A to point B and look for alternatives, we begin finding solutions to our problems. While we are in the process of exploring alternatives, there are no right or wrong answers. If you allow yourself to look at your business this way, a host of alternatives open up. Perhaps in the end you will still choose to go from point A to point B by the most direct and obvious path, but that choice will emerge as a result of exploring many other possibilities.

■ Romancing the Lemon

What amazing creatures we human beings are. Like snowflakes, no two of us are exactly alike. Every person in your company is unique. Each brings individual experiences, talents, ideas, and perspectives to the table. And that's as it should be, up to a point. An Olympic rowing team is also a collection of unique individuals, but all of them are rowing in the same direction with absolute precision.

Is your team rowing in the same direction? Can you be sure everyone is on the same team? Does everyone agree on what your company stands for and what its mission is? Does everyone agree on the company's goals and how to achieve them? Don't be too sure. People seldom agree on the nature of the simplest object—such as a lemon, let alone the nature and objectives of a complex business organization. Try an experiment we call *Romancing the Lemon* at your next meeting with your colleagues. You will need:

1. A lemon.
2. Paper and pencils for each of your colleagues.
3. Fifteen minutes of uninterrupted time.

Ask each person to examine the lemon and write a description of it. Write your own description, too. Some people will give a one-sentence definition, others will write pages. Then ask the group to read back their descriptions. Some will characterize the lemon as a yellow oval; others, as an acidic fruit with an aromatic rind that grows on the citrus limonia native to Asia. Still others will focus on the texture or the Sunkist brand stamped in green. No two people will give the same description.

There's nothing wrong with diversity of opinion or individuals who bring varied perspectives to the company. But once those individuals begin representing your company out in the universe, each must agree exactly on what kind of lemon they are looking at. One of the most important keys to strategic marketing is getting *everyone* to look at your company, its mission, and your strategic marketing plan in the same way. Until everyone is going in the same direction, little will change.

The Top Line

A VP of sales and a VP of production bring very different interests and talents to a company. A consultant and a company veteran will have dissimilar expectations of the company. Even so, each must be on the same team working toward the same objectives. Once everyone is on the same track, creativity and individual talents can be channeled into building a shared vision of the company. And that requires a well-articulated company mission statement.

There's a tremendous bonus in this shared vision. It's called *empowerment*. Making every executive part of the team gives each a greater sense of value. When a company lets its people know that individual efforts and ideas are appreciated and worthwhile, morale and productivity rise exponentially. People at every level begin assuming greater responsibility and enjoying it.

■ Telescope on Today

As executives we are often so deeply immersed in day-to-day activities that thinking clearly about our long-term direction becomes difficult. We do what we must to get the supply lines flowing and profits up—quarter by quarter. Even when we find the time to look ahead and do some long-range planning, our minds are still stuck in the present. It's as if we were looking at our universe through a microscope and missing the big picture.

Worse yet, we see the future as an infinite playground of possibilities. There is always time ahead to do the things that didn't get done today. If you prefer to think about it all tomorrow, then please know that while tomorrow never comes, the years 2000, 2010, and 2020 will arrive all too soon. You must plan for the future today, because tomorrow is too late. How do you do this? Trade in that microscope for a telescope by taking yourself out of the present and into the future. What do you need?

1. 15 minutes.
2. Paper and pencil.
3. Your imagination.

Visualize the year 2020. Your company may be 75 years old. You've ripened a bit, too, but you're still hanging in there. Now look back to those good old days at the turn of the millennium. We thought we were pretty sophisticated with those old fax machines and clunky laptop computers. Remember how your employees would actually travel into a central office every day? And that was about the time globalization was just getting started. There certainly were a lot of opportunities back then.

You get the idea. Now ask yourself—what do you wish you had done back at the turn of the millennium? What could you have accomplished in those years? How could you have repositioned your company? What would you have changed about your service or product line, your methods of distribution, your company culture, or your own role in the company? Ask other key executives to try this exercise.

The Top Line

If you get out of your rut, look at your issues from a fresh perspective, and bring distance and objectivity to your thought processes, solutions appear.

These 3 exercises develop ways of thinking that you will utilize in constructing and implementing your strategic marketing plan. To actually get *from here to there* you must have:

1. The ability to bring fresh perspectives to familiar issues.
2. A mutually understood, shared vision of your company and its mission.

3. The willingness and the will to plan objectively for the future.

Those are a just few of the components essential to applying the principles of strategic marketing and planning to your business.

■ So What Is Strategic Marketing?

Modern marketing was born with the simple recognition that the consumer is king or, more likely, queen. One hundred years ago, when most goods and services were scarce, the seller was in charge of the trading relationship. If he manufactured black harnesses, the customer bought black harnesses. If a retailer sold brown wing-tip shoes, customers bought them without argument. As competition grew, the seller had to work harder to capture the buyer's attention. Sales staffs were hired. Advertising became a sophisticated business, and public relations and market research were born. Along with this, came a recognition that the vendor was in service to the consumer. The vendor's responsibility was not only to offer goods and services, but to offer precisely what the consumer wanted, when she wanted it, and where she wanted it.

As the buyer-seller equation shifted, so did our notion of marketing. Originally *marketing* was defined as the buying and selling of goods in the market. We can still find that definition in various dictionaries. In the changing business world, the understanding of marketing expanded to include sales support functions such as advertising, public relations, and promotion along with activities such as trade show participation. In more recent years, the scope of marketing has expanded further to include the four P's—Product, Price, Promotion, and Place—each aimed at providing customers with the goods and services they desire.

Today the textbook definition of marketing has evolved into *strategic marketing and planning*—a totally integrated approach to assessing a business, creating a vision, framing a mission statement, mapping out objectives, and formulating tactics for achieving those objectives. It also encompasses long-range planning and concepts such as unique competitive advantage, micromarketing, and micromerchandising.

While fine in textbook theory, many other facets of a business must be addressed to create a successful strategic plan. For example, the culture of each organization is unique. Because people help create your culture, they are an important part of your strategic direction.

Avenues of distribution, sales, products or services, presentation, operations, logistics, and technology are some of the other critical links that are part of your strategic value chain. Each of these critical links must be analyzed to find competitive advantages and growth potential for your organization. Finally, a shared vision and mutually agreed upon objectives are the drivers that make change possible.

Only when each of these pieces is in place, can you initiate your tactical maneuvers—along with measurements for success and progress—and begin to move your plan and your team forward.

Throughout this book, we will be using a number of related terms. A *strategic marketing plan* is a road map of analytic steps for assessing business issues, setting company objectives, and planning tactics for reaching those objectives. A *strategic maneuver* or *tactic* is the use of a strategic plan for achieving a specific business goal. Strategic maneuvers are also defined as those stratagems intended to destroy an enemy's war-making capacity—fitting for today's and tomorrow's competitive marketplace.

We will also be talking about *strategic planning*, which is the managerial process of matching an organization's resources with its marketing opportunities over the long run. The strategic planning process consists of defining the organization's mission, setting organizational objectives, and selecting strategies and tactics that will enable the organization to reach its goals.

■ Are You Going to Get from Here to There?

A lot of questions and issues need to be addressed to move you through this process. Take the first step by asking yourself the following questions to discover whether you and your company are prepared for the 21st century. Give yourself time to really think about your answers. Answer each question with a yes or no.

1. Are you competing to be an industry front-runner?
   - ❑ Yes
   - ❑ No

2. Do you spend a major portion of your time on external issues rather than your company's internal issues?
   - ❑ Yes
   - ❑ No

3. Is some of your time devoted to considering how the world could be different in five or ten years?
   - ❑ Yes
   - ❑ No

4. Do you spend time conferring with colleagues with the objective of building a shared view of the future?
   - ❑ Yes
   - ❑ No

5. Are you in control of your company's destiny?
   - ❑ Yes
   - ❑ No

6. Imagine that your company closed today. Can you name three things your customers would genuinely miss?
   - ❑ Yes
   - ❑ No

7. Does your company have a reason for existing five years from now?
   - ❑ Yes
   - ❑ No

8. Can you name three key ingredients in building a vision for your company?
   - ❑ Yes
   - ❑ No

9. Do you know what your customers will want in three years?
   - ❑ Yes
   - ❑ No

10. Does your company have a mission?
    - ❑ Yes
    - ❑ No

Scoring: Give yourself 10 points for each "Yes" answer.

100 points	Prepare to profit in the 21st century.
80 to 90 points	Not bad. But not bad isn't good enough. Read on.
40 to 70 points	Alert! Mediocrity won't cut it in the new millennium.
30 points or less	Do you look good in red? You'll soon be wearing it.

How did you do? Are you a marketing maven or a strategic simpleton? We'll discuss your answers later. For now, just remember that it's not where you start but where you finish that counts. With a solid understanding of the principals of strategic marketing you will finish a winner.

The curiosity to find appropriate solutions, to define the issues and to open up vistas that expand your opportunities for change is critical to success. How you answered the ten questions in *Are You Going to Get from Here to There?* says a lot about the state of your curiosity. If you are curious to know more, read on.

2
Where's Your Curiosity?

Habit is a great deadener.

Samuel Beckett, *Waiting for Godot*

What's curiosity got to do with it?" you ask. Doesn't a vision require genius, divine inspiration, or at least a few flashes of brilliance? No! Oh, there's nothing wrong with genius; it served Shakespeare, Beethoven, and Picasso very well. But genius isn't the essential ingredient for marketing your company into the future; curiosity is. Curiosity put to work will unleash all the creativity and imagination you will ever need.

How so? Imagine, you suddenly decided to write a historical novel set in the 17th century. Would you head off to a cabin in Maine, armed only with your word processor, expecting to emerge six months later with a completed manuscript? Chances are you would emerge with nothing more than a terminal case of writer's block.

Suppose instead you set off to the library or the historical society to learn everything you could about the era. You would research, read, and immerse yourself in the history, culture, literature, and art of the period. You would learn what the

15

people of the times ate, drank, wore, and thought. You would come to understand the politics, sexual behaviors, religious beliefs, and social movements of the time. As you learned more about the era, you would begin to enter the minds of the people of the time. Suddenly you would be thinking the way a man or woman of the 17th century thought. Real, three-dimensional characters would emerge. Only then could you begin to imagine and create.

A vision isn't found in a vacuum, whether you are a writer or a business executive. To discover the marketing direction for your company, you use the same process that you would to develop a novel's characters and plot. But instead of exploring the 17th century, you will discover the world that your customer and your company inhabit.

That requires curiosity. Unfortunately, many of us over time become complacent and habit bound. Has your job grown a little stale? Is it the same routine every day? If so, you need to wake up your curiosity—for your own benefit as well as your company's—and discover the challenging and exciting world your company inhabits. Go beyond the four walls of your office and into the real world.

■ Read Creatively

Reading should awaken curiosity, not put us to sleep. Too many executives limit their reading to internal reports and industry trade journals. They focus on ferreting out items about their own companies and their competition. If that describes your reading habits, break out of that box and open your mind to the wider universe of opportunities that reading creatively offers.

Start by aggressively scanning *The Wall Street Journal, Forbes, BusinessWeek, Fortune,* and the business sections of your local newspaper, a major regional paper, and *The New York Times.* Instead of looking for references to your company and your industry, start looking for ideas and trends. How are companies in other industries dealing with problems and opportunities in areas such as distribution, communications, technology, human relations, compensation, and promotion? Go beyond that. Add relevant consumer magazines to your list of subscriptions. Read at least one major computer magazine that is geared to business. Find out what publications your customers read and get subscriptions. For example, if your company makes household cleaning products that are purchased by middle-income women who are focused on the home and family, then you should be aware of what is being talked about in the pages of *Good Housekeeping, Family Circle,* and *Redbook*—at least. If you offer computerized accounting services to businesses, start reading the trade publications your clients read.

Don't stop with publications. Books, music, films, television, and the World Wide Web are all barometers of consumer interests and desires. When movies such as *Forrest Gump,* become blockbusters, they are reaching something inside the hearts and psyches of the public. When a television show such as *E. R.* or *The X-Files* captures the public imagination, we should tune in and learn why. To stay current on those top ten lists, check any major newspaper, such as *The New York Times,* which runs its "Most Wanted" page each Monday in the Business section. Lists include *Variety*'s top grossing films for the previous week, Nielsen Media Research's top ten TV shows along with the top videos, music albums, computer programs, and technology and media stocks. Check the *New York Times' Book Review* section each Sunday for all the best selling fiction and non-fiction books.

And, if you want to see, hear, and read about what is happening right this minute, try "surfing" the Internet. Hot link your way through almost any subject with Web pages that are being updated all the time. The Internet and services such as American Online provide huge quantities of information, including stock quotes, company profiles, economic trend stories, and market reports to audio samples from the latest CDs.

■   Talk to Your Customers and Your Consumers

Get to know your customers up close. If you sell consumer products or services, go with your salespeople to visit your clients or the outlets you sell. Use the opportunity to talk directly with consumers. Contact with consumers is usually filtered through marketing reports from focus groups, mall intercepts, and surveys. Those are all important elements of market research, but can't substitute for direct contact. Many executives, when faced with a real, live consumer, are at a loss. What do you say after you say, "Do you like our product?" Add these questions to your repertoire:

- Why do you buy our product or service?
- How could we improve it?
- Is it always available when you want it?
- Do you think our pricing is fair?
- When you hear our brand name, what do you think of?
- What other brands do you buy?
- Where do you use our product or service? How?
- How does our product or service help you?
- Does anyone else in your family use the product or service?
- Where do you buy the product or service?
- Would you prefer to buy it in a different way or at a different outlet?

Know that knowledge is power. You must gather as much knowledge as possible to gain and keep a competitive edge.

You must know your customers, your competitors, your suppliers, and the world they each inhabit.

In the United States, we like to think about first quarter and second quarter profits along with return on investment (ROI). We don't like to spend time on research and development and looking into the future. We avoid thinking about how the world is going to be different in the next three to five years. But to survive in this increasingly global economy, we need to see how the world is shaping and reshaping, and how global trends affect our business. We then need to take that information and curiosity and share it with our colleagues to create synergies that unleash curiosity in the people we work with each day.

Go back and reread the questions posed in Chapter 1. Use them to unleash your curiosity and find a future for your company. Curiosity will propel you to strive for a reason to exist and to push beyond where you are today. Without curiosity, you won't know what your customers want. And knowing what your customers want and will want three years from now is essential to your ability to plan for the future. Without curiosity, you can not find a vision for the future, a mission for your company, or a reason to exist.

PART II

LINKING THE STRATEGIC VALUE CHAIN

In Part I we discussed how to "think out of the box," unleash your curiosity, and look beyond your four walls to understand the social, economic, political, and cultural trends that impact your business.

In Part II you will learn how to apply this knowledge directly to your business to find your company's competitive advantage and a vision for the future. You will also discover how to assess the effects change will have on every aspect of your business from service and product development and market research to human resources and distribution.

In Chapters 3 through 19, we will explore the *Strategic Value Chain*—all those key pieces or links of your business that you must consider before you can begin making changes. Together we will walk through each of those essential elements.

Because this process does involve every aspect of your business, your investigation of the Strategic Value Chain *must* be a team effort. Begin by looking at each key department that will be affected by changes in your Strategic Value Chain. Then select a person from each department to participate in the process. You may have as many as ten representatives on this Strategic Assessment Team, or as few as three to five in a smaller company. Remember that all key segments of your business must be represented and empowered into the process to create the synergies and dynamics that create change.

As members of this team, everyone has equal status. There is no hierarchy nor are there captains. Participants take off their hats and titles and work as a team. Team members must bring independence, originality, and enthusiasm to the table, and they must leave their negativity at home. You must all understand and obey a few ground rules, including:

1. The statement, "We've never done it this way before," is not allowed.
2. "We don't do it this way." Ditto.
3. No idea is a bad idea.
4. Judgments are not allowed.

When your Strategic Assessment Team is in place, you are ready to take those first important steps into your company's future.

3

How to Find Your Competitive Advantage

LINKS—Leverage Ideas to Navigate Key Strategies

There are no problems that we can not solve together, and very few that we can solve by ourselves.

Lyndon B. Johnson, 36th President
of the United States

With your Strategic Assessment Team assembled and ready to work, you will start marketing your company into the future using a technique that I have called *LINKS*—Leverage Ideas to Navigate Key Strategies. But, before we start the LINKS process, let's take care of some important business. In this chapter and other sections of the book, you will see the term consumer/customer, referring to both consumers and business customers. Many business-to-business operations assume that marketing expertise is only required for selling consumer products. Wrong! All of the exercises in this book, including the LINKS process, are as valuable for an industrial products manufacturer or a service provider as for a retailer or a consumer products company. Strategic marketing principles work for *everyone*.

Each chapter in this section includes at least one action plan called a *Jump Start*. Jump Starts are intended to get you out on the track and moving fast. Whether you are the CEO of a global corporation, the pop in a mom and pop operation, or the head of a midsize company, Jump Starts are an essential part of the process of working through the Strategic Value Chain. Jump Starts make the process real. Do them as a team and get energized.

You will also notice as you go through these next 16 chapters, that some are long and in-depth, while others are brief and uncomplicated. Some strategic links, such as those discussed in "The New Consumerism," "The New Marketing," and "Channel Power: The Big Sell," are undergoing massive changes. We devoted many pages to those links. Other chapters such as "Training: The Continuous Tool" and "Measurements for Success—Is the Team Meeting Its Goals?" are short. They are included as separate chapters to be sure each link in the Strategic Value Chain has its own thought process and its own Jump Start.

■ Let's Start LINK-ing

The LINKS process demonstrates that cause and effect is not a simple, linear relationship and that an action does not cause a single reaction, but many reactions, which in turn create many other reactions. That's one big reason that LINKS can be put into practice only through team effort. So, is everyone in place? Let's go!

As part of the LINKS process, you will be making lists and drawing. If you are running through the process with a team of three or four members, legal pads and pencils will do. If you are working with a larger team, you will need a large marker board or flip chart with lots of paper. You will also need marking pens.

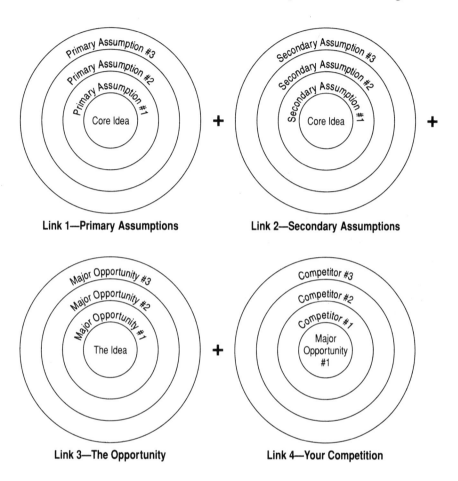

Link 1—Primary Assumptions   Link 2—Secondary Assumptions

Link 3—The Opportunity   Link 4—Your Competition

= A VISION

Exhibit 3–1
The Formula

LINKS is a 4-link, or 4-step, 4 × 4 process (see Exhibit 3–1) that begins with a *core idea* for change and then builds, link by link, until you find your company's competitive advantage and its vision for the future. Your core idea must be:

- *Very specific.* No generalities, vagueness, or wishful thinking, please. Start with a well-defined core idea that can be expressed in a simple sentence. Asking, for example, "What would happen if we advertised more?" is not a core idea. It does not specify how much you will advertise, where you will advertise, or even if you should advertise more. "What would happen if we hired an agency to handle our advertising business?" is an explicit idea you can work with.

  "What if we cut back on promotional expenses?" is just a vague thought, but "What if we eliminate our public relations department and hire an agency?" is an idea. "What would happen if we got involved in higher technology?" is vague, but "What would happen if we instituted e-mail," is specific.

- *Connected to your existing business.* Remember that successful strategic marketing is evolutionary, not revolutionary. The idea must have roots in your existing business, or it won't grow. The core idea of hiring an agency to handle your advertising assumes that you have been advertising and that you have products or services that may need to be advertised. It also assumes that you communicate with your customers, but that you want to find a more effective way to go about it.

Once you have chosen your core idea, you are ready to begin Link 1. Start by listing everything you assume might happen—good or bad—as a result of instituting the core idea. These are *primary assumptions.* You may list as many assumptions as you want. The assumptions can be negative as well as positive. For example, if you were exploring the idea of hiring an advertising agency, one of the primary assumptions linked to the core idea could be "We will gain a more objective view of where we should place our advertising." But you could also list, "An agency may be more costly than an in-house advertising department." Continue listing assumptions, then score them, giving 5 points to the most likely assumption; 1 point to the least likely. Then draw a circle, like those shown in Exhibit 3–1, with the core idea in the center. Draw a larger circle around the first circle and write in your most likely primary assumption. Continue adding concentric circles until you have listed all your key primary assumptions, with the least likely assumption in the circle the furthest away from the core.

Link 1

In working through Link 1, keep in mind five basic precepts:

- Your idea must be very specific.
- Your idea must be connected to your existing business.
- All ideas and possibilities are valid . . . but must be specific.
- An assumption can be positive or negative.
- There is no set number of ideas or assumptions.

Link 2 asks, "What could happen after a primary assumption is instituted?" Consider how the primary assumptions could affect your business. These effects are *secondary assumptions.* For example, if your company did gain a more objective view of where its advertising should be placed, what would happen as a result? A secondary assumption might be that your company would save money choosing more effective media. List your secondary assumptions, and again build circles of secondary assumptions around a core idea.

Link 3 explores the *major opportunities* that may arise as a result of the primary and secondary assumptions. If you did save money by choosing more effective advertising media, what opportunities does that open up? One major opportunity could be increased sales or increased profits on existing sales.

Link 4 looks at your *competition* by connecting your major opportunities to the competitive realities of your industry. In Link 4 you examine where your competition is in relation to your major opportunity. You do not look at your competitors to copy them, but to learn from them so you can better assess your own efforts. Out of this assessment arises an understanding of your company's competitive advantage vis à vis your industry.

To make this process easier, let's use a familiar example—the fax machine. Why the fax machine? Because you have already been through the process. You "pre-understand" it. Whether you adopted this new technology early or waited, you went through a decision-making process in which you debated the pros and cons of the fax machine and considered the ramifications for your business.

The year is 1980 and you own a small publishing company specializing in trade magazines. You've recently been hearing how fax machines will one day be an essential part of any office. Of course, you know that newspaper publishers have been using facsimile machines for years to transmit photographs. But those machines were slow and expensive. However, your editorial and advertising departments could both benefit from faster communications, so it's worth exploring.

Primary Assumptions—Link 1 (Exhibit 3–2)

A core idea emerges: We will install a fax machine in our company headquarters. What could happen if we do? The idea of installing a fax is specific and fits in with your need to communicate with your printers and writers. It could be a step in speeding up your business. What are the assumptions that can arise from this idea? Begin by listing all the

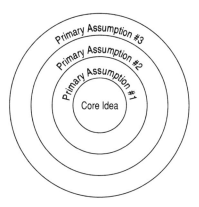

Exhibit 3–2
Primary Assumptions

possibilities that could result, *both positive and negative.* For example:

- We could receive articles from our writers faster.
- Our editors, in turn, could get copy to the printers faster.
- Our production manager could send layout changes to the printer when they happen.
- We could fax advertising information, layouts, and contracts to our customers.
- If we also install a fax in our West Coast office, we can share information more readily.
- We can minimize miscommunications. Things will be in black and white.
- We will save time and money spent on those long phone calls.
- We'll cut down on expenses for overnight packages. And my secretary won't have to make all those late trips to the post office for Express Mail.

Don't forget the possible negatives of bringing a fax into your company, including:

- Fax machines aren't all compatible.
- We have to make a fairly big cash outlay.
- We will have to get a dedicated telephone line.
- We may have to convince the printers to get fax machines too. In fact, most companies don't have fax machines.
- What happens if we accidentally fax important documents to the wrong number? There goes our privacy.
- We will have to train our people to operate the fax.
- Reproduction isn't all that great. And we will have too many documents on that slippery thermal fax paper.

Your core idea has generated primary assumptions. Put each of these assumptions in order from most likely to least likely and score them from 5 (for most likely) to 1 (for least likely). Perhaps your writers are missing deadlines and blaming the mail. Eliminating that situation could be the most important assumption. Perhaps communications with your West Coast office have been poor. Changing that situation could be the most important result of installing a fax machine. Now, as in Exhibit 3–2, draw a circle and write the core idea—in this case, "Install a fax machine"—in the center. Add a series of concentric circles with each of the key primary assumptions, starting with the most likely assumption closest to the core idea.

Secondary Assumptions—Link 2 (Exhibit 3–3)

Next ask yourself, "What could happen as the result of each of these primary assumptions?" Let's assume that communicating faster with your advertisers is the most important

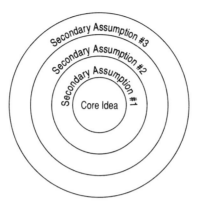

Exhibit 3–3
Secondary Assumptions

and most likely benefit associated with installing a fax. If you have more immediate communications with your ad customers, what could happen? Make a list, again including both positive results and negative results.

- Our sales reps would spend less time trafficking ads and have more time for productive communications with their accounts.
- We could save as much as a week getting approval on ad layouts and copy from out-of-town accounts.
- We could get signatures on advertising contracts more quickly.
- When we come up with an idea for an advertiser, we can get an immediate reaction.

Don't forget the negatives.

- What if we were late getting an ad layout together? We couldn't blame the mails either.

- A faxed contract isn't legally binding. We'd have to get the actual contract in the mail anyway.
- We could lose some of our face-to-face contact with advertisers.

The secondary assumptions grow out of the core idea and the primary assumptions. Score each of these secondary assumptions from 5 points (most likely to occur) to 1 point (least likely), and build your model of concentric circles as in Exhibit 3–3.

Major Opportunities—Link 3 (Exhibit 3–4)

The core idea of installing a fax, matched with the primary and secondary assumptions, leads to the major opportunities—the third link in the expanding ripple effect. You ask, "What happens if we install a fax, which would allow us faster communications with our customers? And what if that communications allowed us to get advertising approval more quickly? What opportunities does that suggest?"

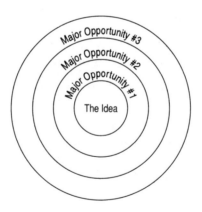

Exhibit 3–4
Major Opportunities

- We can meet our printing deadlines more easily.
- Our sales reps would have more time for prospecting new accounts.
- With faster communications from our advertisers, we can layout the magazines earlier and more accurately and therefore save money on our print bill.
- If we have better control over the advertising function, we can begin to think about new directions for the company.

As in Exhibit 3–4, the opportunities grow out of the core idea and the assumptions. Score the opportunities from 5 (most likely) to 1 (least likely) and then build the model of concentric circles around the core idea.

The Competition—Link 4 (Exhibit 3–5)

Before you run out and order that fax, look at competing publishers. What's are they doing? Are your competitors likely to install a fax or are they still operating at a leisurely

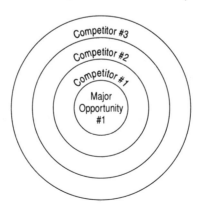

Exhibit 3–5
The Competition

pace? Are they likely to improve their products and services, or can you get the jump on them?

By asking such questions you will link your opportunities with the competition, as in Exhibit 3–5, and discover your competitive advantage. Out of this you will begin to develop a *vision* for your company and find ways to market your company into the future.

■   LINKS Your Company into the Future

Let's move forward in time and apply the process to today's business world. Take this step-by-step again, this time using e-mail as the core idea. Introducing e-mail into your company meets the criteria for a core idea. It is very specific and relates to your existing business. You already communicate using computers, mail, telephones, faxes, and messenger. E-mail is an evolution of those forms of communication.

Primary Assumptions—Link 1 (Exhibit 3–6)

Ask, "What could happen as a result of instituting e-mail?" What assumptions arise as a result? Remember you can list all the positive and negative assumptions that come to mind. This time, write your own list of assumptions, then compare it to the following list.

- Speeds up information to groups and individuals.
- Provides faster answers.
- Facilitates coordination of thought processes.
- Provides better thought leadership.
- Affords better teaming.
- Affords faster and better communications within the company.
- Affords faster and better communications with clients.
- Affords faster and better communications with vendors.

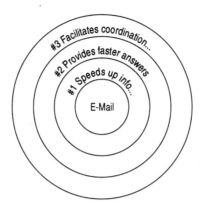

Exhibit 3-6
E-Mail Primary Assumptions

Don't forget the negative assumptions of bringing e-mail into your company.

- People will be confused initially. Confusion creates a need for training.
- Messages might get lost on the Internet.
- Security problems may arise.
- Technical problems may arise. Computers crash.

Now score each of your assumptions from 5 (most likely) to 1 (least likely); then give reasons why you have ranked each in a particular position. A company with a history of poor vendor communications may rank "Affords faster and better communications with vendors" high on its list. A company with limited experience with computers and no in-house technical staff, may put "Technical problems may arise. Computers crash." high on its list. A more technically-savvy company would not consider this a priority. Your assumptions will grow out of your core idea as in Exhibit 3-6.

Secondary Assumptions—Link 2 (Exhibit 3–7)

Having scored each of your primary assumptions, let's explore the secondary ripple-effect. What happens as a result of the primary assumptions? Let's begin with "Speeds information to groups and individuals." What would happen if your vice president of sales was able to get information about a product improvement to every sales representative and assistant instantaneously? Here are a few secondary assumptions.

- Saves time required to print and mail memos.
- Saves postage and printing costs.
- Provides sales representatives opportunities to react quickly.
- Allows sales representatives to be more efficient and effective.
- Provides opportunities for more immediate feedback from customers.

Exhibit 3–7
E-Mail Secondary Assumptions

Consider the negatives also:

- There wouldn't be the same opportunities to proofread memos, so misinformation could get out more easily.
- Someone might intercept our memos.
- There are expenses connected with e-mail.

From your own list of primary assumptions, take those you have scored most likely to happen and create a list of secondary assumptions for each. As in Exhibit 3–7, your secondary assumptions grow out of the core idea. When you are finished, score each of the secondary assumptions from 5 (most likely) to 1 (least likely).

You don't have to stop with secondary assumptions. Take the last of the secondary assumptions: "Provides opportunities for more immediate feedback from customers." and follow with additional assumptions.

- Aids in more efficient product and service planning.
- Creates positive feeling between customers and company.
- Speeds company response time.
- Helps minimize costly production mistakes.

What are the negatives of more immediate customer feedback?

- We could be misled by a few highly vocal customers.
- Our designers could become overly dependent on customer feedback and lose creativity.

Major Opportunities—Link 3 (Exhibit 3–8)

Like the ripples created by a single stone, the assumptions continue expanding, constantly creating new assumptions.

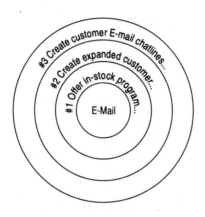

Exhibit 3–8
E-Mail Major Opportunities

From the core idea, the primary assumptions and the secondary assumptions come opportunities.

Just as we have used the "Thinking Out of the Box" process to move from the core idea out toward the assumptions, we will look at the primary and secondary assumptions and ask, "What if we institute e-mail speeding our communications, thereby speeding up consumer feedback? And what if that, in turn, expedites company response time and minimizes costly production mistakes? What major opportunity does all this afford?" Again, be specific and be certain that the opportunities relate to your current business. Some examples could be:

- Offer an in-stock program of "customers' choice products" for fast delivery.
- Create an expanded customer service program.
- Create customer e-mail chatlines dealing with various products and services.
- Create an e-mail order system.

Once again, rank the opportunities from 5 (most likely) to 1 (least likely), then draw the model of concentric circles as in Exhibit 3–8.

The Competition—Link 4 (Exhibit 3–9)

Before you begin developing these opportunities, look at your industry. What is your competition doing or not doing in these areas? Are they already using e-mail and how effectively? Are they already involved in the major opportunity areas? If so, how well are they doing?

Link up the major opportunity with the competition, as in Exhibit 3–9, and ask yourself:

- How do we compare?
- How do we perceive our competition vs. these major opportunities?

By matching the opportunities with the competition, you will find your competitive advantages and arrive at a *vision*

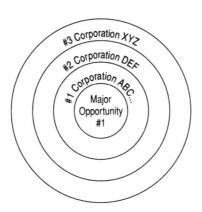

Exhibit 3–9
E-Mail the Competition

for your company. You will understand what opportunities exist for you and what your competition is doing or not doing, or is likely to do, or not do, in those areas. As you analyze these opportunities a vision for your company will begin to materialize. You will see a future for your company and can begin to market your company into that future.

■ Linking Together the Strategic Value Chain

You've learned how to think out-of-the-box and muster your curiosity. Through the LINKS process, you've discovered visions for new opportunities. Now it's time to apply this to each of the key links in your business—your Strategic Value Chain. These links may vary somewhat from company to company, but will certainly include such areas as corporate culture, sales, marketing, operations, technology, human resources, distribution and products or services—all of the areas included in Chapters 4 through 19.

Before the era of strategic marketing, we tended to think of company departments as separate entities—one often in competition with the other. Division heads were frequently territorial and competitive, jealously guarding the boundaries of their departments. To survive in the next millennium, companies must throw off the mantel of territoriality and build relationships or links between each of their divisions and functions. The Strategic Value Chain calls for a holistic approach to business with an open flow of communications from each business segment into the next. Without this flow, you can not build for the future.

That is one of the important reasons for choosing representatives from each key department to lead the strategic planning process. The formation of the Strategic Assessment Team not only empowers the entire company to become involved in the procedure but assures that no facet of your business is overlooked along the way. In addition, the team approach is more likely to encourage long-term thinking, rather than preoccupation with individual departments' short-term goals.

The technology link, which we discuss in Chapter 14, "Real Time," demonstrates the importance of each area of the company working interdepartmentally to achieve goals. Technology is a major enabler that speeds information within your company and to your customer. Technology and its systems are interactive links to every other link in the Strategic Value Chain.

Today's customer is demanding faster response to their product, service, and informational needs. In the process of servicing your customer, the Strategic Value Chain speeds up, creating stress on the various strategic links of your organization. Each of those links will be intermeshed by the technology that is needed to carry information throughout the Strategic Value Chain. A technology department that guards its expertise and information—as many have in the past—is counterproductive in today's business environment.

In the same manner, sales is a critical link that connects to each segment of your business. It must provide a constant flow of shared information. The sales department must understand its place within the company and the importance of its relationships to marketing, production, distribution, technology, and other links. The traditionally adversarial relationships between sales and other functions, such as production, have always been counterproductive. They certainly have no place in the 21st century. Tomorrow's sales department will work as partners with their customers, using new technology, such as laptop computers, to share information and link their customers to the company in real time. Tomorrow's sales department will, in effect, become a communications department.

As we move through the next 16 chapters, we will explore how each segment and function of your business is linked to the next, and how those interactions are empowered by your people.

Exhibit 3–10
Blast Off!

Think now of these links, the Strategic Value Chain, as a rocket ship about to blast off such as the one in Exhibit 3–10. Most of us are not rocket scientists, but we all understand that each piece of a rocket ship interacts with the other. If one piece does not fit, the rocket ship goes nowhere. We also know that without fuel a rocket ship never gets off the ground. In order to propel our rocket ship into space, we must consider what kind of energy moves and motivates our business. That energy is people. People truly move our business toward:

- New ideas.
- Increased sales growth.
- Improved profitability.

Your people working together push ideas to the top. They provide the impetus to grow your sales and your profits. Traditionally profits were your bottom line. But in our rocketship the efforts of your people, working throughout each of the strategic links, push gross margins and revenue enhancements to the *top,* making your profits your *top line.*

As we move into the individual links of the Strategic Value Chain, you will see how these pieces of your business mesh together to formulate a strategy that will market your company into the future. You cannot begin to move into the future without a corporate vision. Using the LINKS process, you have learned how new opportunities, placed in the context of your competitive environment, can lead to visions for your company's future. In the next chapter, you will use the results of the LINKS exercises to build a vision statement that will be the first link in your Strategic Value Chain and the first piece of the rocketship (see Exhibit 3–11) that will propel you, your team and your company into a profitable future.

Measurements
for Control

Measurements
for Success—
Goal Tracking

The Top Line

Training

Right Place

Real Time

Channel Power

Product/Service

New Marketing

New Consumerism

Operations

Organization

Infrastructure

Culture Factor

Mission

Vision

Exhibit 3–11
The Links

4

The Vision Thing

Vision is the art of seeing things invisible.

Jonathan Swift, *Thoughts on Various Subjects*

George Bush never figured out "the vision thing." Bill Clinton did, at least for a while, but Bob Dole's seemed fuzzy at best. Having a vision may not be enough to get one elected president of the United States, but it sure helps. Few people are willing to give their votes to an individual who cannot envision and articulate a better world and a better way to reach that world.

A company and its employees need a reality-based vision just as a presidential candidate does. But what is a vision, anyway? The *American Heritage Dictionary* defines vision as "unusual competence in discernment or perception, intelligent foresight." *Webster's Dictionary* defines vision as "the act or power of anticipating that which will or may come to be, foresight, entrepreneurial vision."

A *vision* is a statement of purpose and philosophy that empowers and guides everyone throughout your company. A *vision statement* says,

> This is what we want to be as a company. And this is how we behave in achieving our goals.

45

The well-crafted vision statement will be specific enough to serve as a guidepost, but not so specific that it deters company members from taking initiative and assuming decision-making power.

A vision statement is the broad, lofty, but unequivocal expression of what you and your strategic marketing team agree your company *could* and *can be.* For example, one vision statement reads, "Worldwide Widgets is an integrated company dedicated to serving its customers' needs and functioning as a good neighbor in its business community." This vision statement was reached after collectively studying the opportunities and competitive realities the company faced. It does not touch upon actual arenas of business or channels of distribution, nor does it give details of what the company does—that comes later in the mission statement. But it does state clearly that the company puts the customer first and that its behavior should never compromise the welfare of the community.

Consider also the vision statement of a midsize consumer products company with retail outlets and manufacturing facilities in various areas of the country. This company, which went through the process of a strategic marketing assessment, had no prior vision. After the assessment, the company's strategic assessment team agreed on the following:

> We are a market-driven company dedicated to quality in all our endeavors.

The statement reflected the team's determination to transform the company from a production-driven operation to a consumer-oriented firm. The statement was also aimed at emphasizing their determination to improve quality of product and service.

If the concept of a vision still seems like a bit vague, consider these very specific visions of several world class companies:

Microsoft: A computer on every desk and in every home.

General Motors: GM's vision is to be the world leader in transportation products and related services. We will earn our customers' enthusiasm through continuous improvement driven by the integrity, teamwork, and innovation of GM people.

Wendy's International: To be the customer's restaurant of choice, the employer of choice, and the franchiser of choice.

Mobil Corporation: To be a great, global company. A company, built with pride by all our people, that sets the standard for excellence. A company that brings value to our customers, provides superior returns to our shareholders, and respects the quality of life in every one of our communities.

Reynolds Metals Company: We the men and women of Reynolds Metals Company, are dedicated to being the premier supplier and recycler of aluminum and other products in the global markets we serve.

Each of these companies is global. But vision and mission statements are just as important to companies with more limited territories. An example is Niagara Mohawk Power Corp. Its vision reads:

We will become the most responsive and efficient energy services company in the Northeast and the energy supplier of choice in a more competitive environment.

■ Living the Vision

A vision statement, like any philosophy, only has value if it is lived day by day. It begins as an abstract idea and becomes real as it is put into practice. Compromising your vision for the sake of short-term expediency is as bad as having no vision at all. So take every opportunity to demonstrate to customers and employees that your vision is alive and shining clearly.

The process of creating a vision is also valuable in developing a true team climate. It gives team members from finance, sales, production, distribution, and other key functions an opportunity to focus on the company as a whole and work together to redirect the company. The work your team devotes to the vision prepares them for the cooperative effort ahead as they formulate or revise your company's mission statement and objectives and assess each of the links in the Strategic Value Chain.

JUMP START . . . .

Of course, you want to begin working on your strategic assessment now. The Jump Starts located in each of the chapters of Part II provide three or four easy steps that will put you and your strategic assessment team right on track. Remember that every step in the strategic assessment is a team effort.

To get a Jump Start on creating your Vision Statement . . . .

1. After completing the LINKS process, ask each team member what he or she believes your company should and can be.

2. Assign people from your strategic assessment team to write the Vision Statement. If you have a large team, ask three or four members to work on the wording. If you have a smaller team, let everyone work on it.

3. Review the statement with your team and rewrite it until you have a mutually agreed upon vision.

5

Mission Possible

It is not enough to aim, you must hit.

Italian proverb

Once you have created your vision statement, you are ready to focus on your company's *mission statement.* Your vision states what you believe your company *can be;* the mission statement is related to what you expect to *achieve.* The creation of a mutually agreed upon mission is one of the most critical steps in the Strategic Value Chain. The mission statement's wording defines how you and everyone within the firm sees the company and its role in the business universe.

A mission statement *broadly* defines the company's arena of business, its customers, and its objectives for the future, usually in five sentences or less. If the mission statement is written too broadly, it will offer little direction or sense of identity. If written too narrowly, it will limit the firm's horizons.

If you and your team are creating a mission statement for the first time, realize that it's one of the first steps a company must take when it is shifting directions or widening its scope. If you already have a mission statement, be aware that you may have to rework it to focus your employees on the changes you expect to make.

As companies move forward in this process, they may choose to bring in a facilitator to assist in the strategic planning process. A neutral, objective person, who is trained in the thinking process, can help pull the strategic marketing team together and keep the planning process moving more quickly.

Compare a "before" and "after" mission statement from the midsized manufacturer of consumer products whose vision statement was discussed in Chapter 4. Their before statement read:

> Our mission is to meet the challenges of an ever-changing market place. We are committed to the production and sale of well-designed and reasonably priced quality merchandise. It is our obligation to our customers, shareholders and employees to ensure future growth by continuous improvement to our process and product. To accomplish this, each employee from corporate management to production worker must be a committed member of our quality team.

After analyzing the company's current product mix, sales, and distribution, along with the company's opportunities and its competitive position in the marketplace, a broader mission statement was recommended. A statement that focused less on producing and selling goods and more on responsiveness to customer needs could open up new opportunities.

The revised mission statement reads:

> To create an integrated company, responsive to market changes, with a common goal of profitability and sales growth focused across all lines of business.

By focusing on this mission statement, the company would be better able to develop into a marketing driven company, to create a single company culture, and to respond to the changing consumer in a more timely manner. The statement was also aimed at spurring diversification of retail distribution and product lines, increasing distribution, and establishing new lines of business.

The mission statement is essential in empowering people throughout the organization. That empowerment, however, is not achieved by demanding employee commitment, as the "before" mission statement sought to do, but by involving representatives from the various segments of the Strategic Value Chain in the actual formulation of the statement to create the synergies and dynamics that effect change. It also empowers your people by presenting a statement that focuses employees on the company's goals. The mission statement helps keep everyone rowing in the same direction. Employees should refer to the company's mission statement regularly and use it as a guide.

Consider how a chain of women's beauty salons reformulated their mission statement to put the customer first and to encompass a broader range of services. The original statement read:

> XYZ Salons, Inc. is dedicated to offering the latest hairstyling and makeup techniques. Our modern facilities, experienced stylists, and management expertise assure that XYZ is the top salon in every location.

Compare that to this statement:

> XYZ Salons is committed to offering complete salon services that meet our customers' changing beauty and body care needs. The hallmarks of XYZ Salons—the expertise of our personnel, our quality environments, and an emphasis on customer service—enable us to meet our twin goals of increased sales and profitability.

What do major corporations incorporate into their mission statements? Here are a few examples:

AT&T: We are dedicated to being the world's best at bringing people together—giving them easy access to each other and to the information and services they want and need—anytime, anywhere.

Sara Lee: Sara Lee Corporation's mission is to build leadership brands in consumer packaged goods markets around the world. Our primary purpose is to create long-term stockholder value.

How do some of the giants' mission statements compare with their visions? As you read in Chapter 4, Wendy's International, the world's third largest burger chain, succinctly set its vision on being the restaurant and the employer of choice. Its mission is also direct:

- Deliver to the customer a satisfying experience.
- Create the Wendy's difference.
- Grow a healthy system.
- Foster a performance driven culture.

Compare also Mobil Corporation's broad and lofty vision statement on page 47 with its mission which more closely defines the company's business and its objectives for the future.

To be a dynamic company that will continually find and develop opportunities for profitable growth in our core businesses, and that will realize the greatest value from our existing assets while keeping tight control of our costs.

Compare too the vision of Reynolds Metals Company on page 47 with its mission statement:

Working together, our mission is to provide our customers with uncompromising quality, innovation, and continuous improvement, which will result in the profitable growth and financial strength of our company.

Company objectives are an integral part of the mission statement. These must be broad enough to allow room for growth. For example, a well-worded objective for an aeronautics company might be: "We aim to maintain a competitive advantage by designing the best products in aerospace." On the other hand, "In six months we will have a revolutionary engine that will utilize 50 percent less gas," is far too narrow and specific to belong in a mission statement or be part of a company's objectives.

Formulate no less than six and no more than ten objectives that can be related to any link of the Strategic Value Chain—technology, customer service, product/service, distribution, or any other segment of the business. Taking a team approach helps assure that all segments of your company will pull together to realize their mutually conceived objectives.

JUMP START . . . .

1. Using your vision statement as a starting point, discuss and try to agree on various elements of the company's mission.

2. Have each member submit and discuss objectives that he or she feels should be incorporated into the company's list of objectives. Then discuss with the team.

3. As with the vision statement, assign team members to write the first draft of your mission statement and objectives.

4. Review and rewrite until you have a mission and objectives that everyone agrees upon and endorses enthusiastically.

6

The Culture Factor

Most of the things we do, we do for no better reason than that our fathers have done them or our neighbors do them, and the same is true of a larger part than what we suspect of what we think.

Oliver Wendell Holmes, Jr., Boston speech, 1897

We often think of culture as the highest artistic and intellectual expressions of society—the Joffrey Ballet, the Metropolitan Opera, the Philadelphia Philharmonic, and the National Gallery of Art. But great literature and fine art are just one side of culture. All people—and companies—develop a culture over time, although most of the expressions of those cultures are never going to make it to a symphony hall or museum. *Webster's Dictionary* defines culture as "the behaviors and beliefs characteristic of a particular social, ethnic, or age group." Wherever there are institutions or groups of people with a commonality, a culture develops, and businesses are not exceptions.

The finest vision and the best-crafted mission statement can be undone by a contrary corporate culture. The deeply ingrained habits and attitudes of management and its employees must be recognized and dealt with before a company can begin to pursue its objectives. Unlike a piece of machinery or a bad ad campaign, you can't just scrap a corporate culture and start over. That culture is a very powerful intangible that must be changed piece by piece. If the whole task seems insurmountable, there are even corporate culture specialists who will examine your culture and help facilitate change.

In Chapter 5, we presented two mission statements from a company that undertook a strategic assessment. One of that company's big problems was a "can't do" and a "we don't do it that way" corporate culture. Faced with news of reorganization, many employees were highly skeptical. Some of their comments included:

- "Corporate asks, but they don't listen. The company doesn't follow through on anything."
- "We don't know what is expected of us."
- "I'm always putting out fires . . . there are no reports for me to use to identify potential problems."
- "No one can ever make a decision . . . it always requires follow-up calls."

Does any of this sound familiar? Is your company resistant to change? Is there a feeling of inflexibility or a mind set that says, "We are going to do it the way we did it before?" Then your must make a concentrated effort to alter your corporate culture. Since much of the culture is a result of how the top three or four people interact with each other, it cannot change without the example of those executives.

A negative corporate culture is often the result of too little communication. Most executives are great at sending down directives, but few have systems for getting feedback from the bottom up. Top management must know what their employees are thinking, just as they need to know what their customers are thinking. The culture factor cannot be changed by directing employees to be more committed or more enthusiastic. It can only be changed by example, action, and team work. Forming your strategic assessment team is a step forward.

Practicing and encouraging open communications interdepartmentally is also essential. If the links of the Strategic Value Chain are blocked, if one department thinks of itself as an independent agent, then the flow of continuous information is impeded and a team effort becomes impossible.

Before you can change your corporate culture, you must look at the various elements that constitute it:

- *The age of the company.* A younger company is usually more open to change than a firm with a 100-year tradition.

- *Location.* Is your company in a small town, a suburb, or a big city? Location makes a big difference in employee and management expectations.

- *History.* Is your company family-owned, public, or multigenerational?

- *How fast has your company grown?* Rapid growth is usually associated with a more flexible corporate culture. With the infusion of new people, a rigid corporate culture doesn't have time to form.

- *Dynamics of dress code.* Is business attire expected for executives? Do you have dress down days?

- *The work ethic.* Do employees frequently work late or on weekends? Is the person who is still at his desk at 10 PM considered a real worker, or someone who can't get his job done on time?

- *How are people treated by the management of the organization?* What do you really think of your employees? Are they your most important asset or just cogs in a machine? You can't hide how you feel about your employees.

- *Does the company respect its customers?* Respect for customers comes from the top. If you don't have it, find new customers or expect to go out of business.

- *Ethics, integrity.* Do you have a written set of business ethics? Where can your employees turn if they are uncertain of how to behave in a given situation? A company that expects a certain level of integrity from its employees has a very different culture than one that expects its employees to do whatever is necessary to make a sale.

- *How are people rewarded in the company?* Are employees paid straight salaries? Do you give merit raises? Are major bonuses awarded at the end of the year? Are benefits generous? Are perks and privileges limited to upper management?

- *How do your people communicate?* Is open communication encouraged throughout the company? It can make all the difference in a corporate culture.

All of these elements must be addressed before you can hope to affect real change. You must ask yourself: What the are needs of the corporate culture? What must be different before the company can move forward? Without flexibility, the right attitude, and management's commitment, nothing else will change in the company. Just remember, change starts at the top.

JUMP START . . . .

1. Using the list of the culture factor elements in this chapter (age of company, work ethic, etc.) build a corporate culture profile for your company.

2. Discuss how each element of your corporate culture helps or hinders your pursuit of your mission and objectives.

3. Create an action plan for adapting your corporate culture to your mission and objectives.

7
Infrastructure

Framework for the Future

Keep in mind always the present you are constructing. It should be the future you want.

Alice Walker, Pulitzer Prize winning author
of *The Color Purple*

Like every other aspect of your business, your infrastructure must present your customer or client with an image that is consistent across all lines of the business. To enable this process and to plan efficiently, the scope of the *single business units* (SBUs) and other departments must be well defined. The SBUs activities must accommodate the corporate vision and mission, as well as the corporate short- and long-term objectives. It should have authority and control over its strategic plans and should be accountable for its results.

In a bottom-up approach, the product/market units must first be defined to ensure they tie in with the company's mission. A top-down approach can also be used to determine whether the firm is large and diverse enough to justify organizing separate

SBUs. An SBU must generate a rather large profit to justify its creation.

The objectives of the SBU should be merged with the expectations of the corporate executives. The goals of the SBU should also be substantially homogeneous and fit strategically with the corporation's overall strategies. For a strong, tied-together infrastructure, several common factors and questions must be addressed:

- Are there common technologies among units?
- Are there common production or distribution facilities?
- Is there a common brand name?
- Is there joint use of the sales force and are they in place to:

  Build market share?

  Maintain market share?

  Harvest?

  Divest?

Once you have considered these factors, you can analyze the operation's costs to find ways to provide more, better, and faster value to your customers, and do it for less—again, a "thinking out of the box" mentality.

JUMP START . . . .

1. Create a chart listing your company's SBUs or departments from top to bottom.
2. Across the top of the chart list all the common factors these SBUs might share (common production, sales force, distribution, image, etc.).
3. Discuss any disconnects in your infrastructure and how you can work to improve the homogeneity of the overall organization.

8
The Organization

The people, and the people alone, are the motive force in the making of world history.

Mao Zedong, *Quotations from Chairman Mao Zedong*

Once you are satisfied that you have a solid infrastructure in place, you must examine your company's organization in human terms to see if that structure can accommodate the changes and the objectives you are pursuing. You must look at your chain of command and organization chart to be sure you are optimally structured. Then, you must consider whether you have enough people and the right people in place throughout the organization.

While your strategic assessment team and other executives are dealing with the broader strategies, most of your organization will be involved in the tactical maneuvers—the specific nitty-gritty, how-tos of getting your ideas and objectives accomplished. Your organization will detail out the what, where, when, how, and who.

However, even the most well-funded company isn't able to accommodate all the changes at one time. You must set priorities. Your best option is to·

accomplish goals in strategic pieces, so that each piece links into the next to create the progressions for change.

People make it happen, and you must be certain you have enough people in critical areas. More importantly, you must also have the right people with the right skills and the right thought leadership to accomplish your objectives. You already took the first step when you brought together your strategic assessment team. As you meet with them to examine the Strategic Value Chain and assess your direction, you will decide how well your organization currently accommodates the direction you want to take. It's important in any reorganization to keep the focus on the customer or consumer. Remember that any reengineering should aim to better service the customer, client, or consumer. Are your people placed where they can best serve the needs of your client or consumer?

Reengineering doesn't necessarily mean turning your company upside down. For example, assume that you have only one person in your technology department, but your strategies call for strong technological expertise. If so, expanding your technology department is a critical success factor in making your strategies work. You might add people to that department or hire a more sophisticated person to either replace or come in over the person who is presently there. The person you put into that key spot must have the right thought leadership and skills and must understand how to work with the other links to create success.

As you go through the strategic links in the following chapters, you will look again at how your organization is structured in terms of departments, departmental leadership, and the flow of information among the departments. Information must flow back and forth from department to department and from top to bottom and back up. You must create an organization chart that will communicate to everyone the chain of command, the flow of information, and the reorganized structure. Everyone must have a road map that shows where to go and who to see for information and direction. People also need an organization chart to know where they fit within that organization.

Exhibit 8–1 shows an example of traditional organizational structure for a consumer products company or manufacturer. Each of the company's functions seem isolated. After a strategic assessment, the organization chart was redesigned to de-emphasize the corporate reporting structure and emphasize flow process from the supplier to the consumer (see Exhibit 8–2).

Small to midsize companies in which "everyone knows what they are doing" can also benefit from organization charts that reflect the desired company structure. Exhibit 8–3 shows the original organization chart for a midsize service company. In this traditional chart, each of the four departments is an isolated entity reporting up to the president/marketing manager. Exhibit 8–4 indicates a more open flow of communication between the departments and the president/marketing manager. The layout also indicates a less rigid hierarchy.

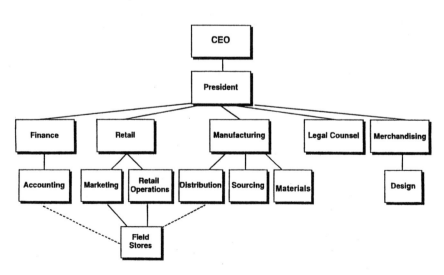

Exhibit 8–1
Consumer Products Company (before)

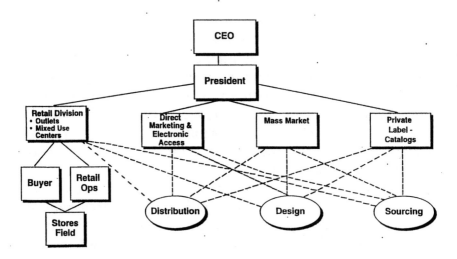

Exhibit 8–2
Consumer Products Company (after)

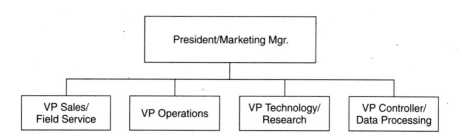

Exhibit 8–3
Small to Mid-Size Company (before)

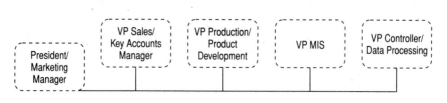

Exhibit 8–4
Small to Mid-Size Company (after)

Often, an executive's biggest mistake is failing to thoroughly think through the organization's structure. Never assume that the old structure or existing personnel can handle the new strategies with a little patching and tweaking. Failing to realize that the top executives only truly take control when they are willing to share power is another major, but common, mistake. When power is in the hands of a few, rather than shared throughout the organization, communications shuts down. Departments become territorial and jealously guard their power and information.

Reengineering begins with the strategic assessment team. By empowering your people, you have set an example for shared power. They will now help create the organization chart that will help make change work. Their insights into what organizational changes must be made to meet your new strategic plans is essential. But if the decision-making process is kept in the hands of a few as opposed to a team, nothing will happen. Your people won't buy into any change that they don't believe recognizes the real needs of the organization.

JUMP START . . . .

Using your current organization chart as a point of departure, ask your team to assess:

1. Which departments they must communicate with regularly to realize your mission and objectives.

2. How much and what type of people power they need to realize their departments' and the company's mission and objectives.

3. Discuss how you could change your current organization to better serve the customer and meet your mission and objectives.

9

Operations

A Strategic Tool

God is in the details.

Mies van der Rohe, German-born
American architect

No strategic marketing plan can work without attention to *operations* and its role in the Strategic Value Chain. Is your company's operations consistent with your vision, mission, and objectives? Or is there a breakdown at the operations level?

What constitutes operations? Operations, for consumer products manufacturers, service providers, and retailers alike, includes all the activities involved in the selling of the product or service up to the taking of payment from the client, customer, or consumer. Operations, rather than planning, is the principle concern of single business unit (SBU) managers. The SBU's planning decisions are made in coordination with corporate plans. Their administration of operational duties must also be in coordination with corporate strategies.

Operations can also be a key factor in differentiation strategies. If you are a retailer, for example, does your operations say "off-price" or "discount"? Does it offer a "no frills" environment with little or no sales assistance? Or is your operations consistent with upscale retailing. Does it rely heavily on display and sales assistance? The many details that go into creating your overall operations are a major factor in differentiating the two types of retailers.

Likewise, consumer products companies, manufacturers, and service providers can use the elements of operations strategically. Consider, for example, the operations of IBM with its global sales and service organization, top-of-the-line facilities, and extensive television and print advertising and promotional programs. It sends a far different message to its customers than does the operations of a low margin, mail-order computer company, which interfaces with customers on-line, by telephone, and through print ads in specialized publications.

Inventory management is an important piece of operations for any business. A major cost driver, it identifies slow-moving items for markdowns and fast-moving items for reorders timed to prevent stockouts.

Operations also encompasses your production and warehousing facilities, office space, security systems, maintenance, office equipment, and supplies. Each of the choices made in these areas must be aligned with the company's strategic needs and the needs of each of the departments that operations serves. Whether you are a manufacturer, retailer, or service provider, you and your operations personnel should consider the following questions:

- Does your operations present a homogeneous image that's indicative of the customer you are trying to reach?

- Are your format, fixturing, and displays consistent with that image?

- Is product arrival consistent?
- Do your plan-o-grams (layouts for product and fixturing) really work?
- Do your product lines flow?
- Is everyone in operations on the same wavelength?

If you are a service provider, you should also consider the following:

- Do your services complement one another?
- Do they send a message to the customer or client that is consistent with your company image?
- Do your collateral materials reinforce that message?
- Do your services further your vision, mission, and objectives?

As with other links in the Strategic Value Chain, communications is essential to operations. You can improve and institute new channels of communications by:

- Developing an internal newsletter communicating service, product, policy, and operational information.
- Soliciting feedback from personnel throughout operations.
- Developing training programs related to service and product knowledge.
- Expanding MIS capabilities to ensure a flow of information through operations and between operations and other segments of the company.

Maintaining cost effectiveness in each of the various pieces of the operation is vital. Examining how structure and expenses can be re-engineered to maintain efficiency, service, and other factors critical to the strategic process is very important.

Sometimes, indeed many times, you need to look at how your customers see your operations and infrastructure and what that means financially. A root cause analysis can help prioritize the problem areas and help you decide which to attack first. The infrastructure must then be accommodated with human resources management. The organizational skills required to manage a complex business must match those of your people. Don't forget that your people have a major impact on how your concept and strategy develop.

Your organization, infrastructure, and operations provide the framework for your developing strategies. That framework, however, must be built to satisfy the needs of your real CEO—the consumer.

JUMP START . . . .

1. Ask each team member to review and report on how his or her department's operations fit or do not fit the company's mission and objectives.

2. As a group, assess each department's operations in relation to the questions posed in this chapter.

3. Ask team members to assess how better communications can improve their operations.

4. Assign a task force to determine where cost savings can be realized.

10

The New Consumerism

The customer is always right.

H. Gordon Selfridge, American-born British
businessman and founder of Selfridge's, U.K.

In the early 1960s, consumer advocate Ralph Nader made his mark on the public consciousness with *consumerism*—a word that conjured up defenseless consumers pitted against fly-by-night companies and unfeeling corporations. Rereading the headlines from those days suggests that businesses saw their customers as adversaries. The term *consumer advocate* was anathema to even scrupulously honest companies. After all, who were these people meddling in your business? Didn't you know what your customers wanted better than any consumer advocate?

What a difference three decades have made! While some companies still cheat, chisel, or simply ignore the needs of the consumer, they have become far more marginal. Today, aware manufacturers, service companies, retailers, and even business-to-business vendors understand and cater to the needs, interests, buying habits, and lifestyles of their customers. We have entered the age of "the

71

new consumerism" with the company itself functioning as consumer advocate and the consumer installed as the company's CEO.

Whether your company markets directly to consumers or to other businesses, you and everyone in your company ultimately report to your customers. How did that happen? Over the past few decades, the consumer/customer has wrested greater and greater control over decisions companies make regarding what products and services are brought to market and how and when they get there. In the 1950s and 1960s, the customer played a more passive role in the buyer-seller equation. Vendors advertised new products in trade publications to alert customers, hyped their salesforces, then marched their product or service off to market. Everyone in the distribution chain pushed the product through. Inflated inventories just meant everyone had to push a little harder. Long lead times posed few problems; consumers were accustomed to waiting patiently for new products. Since vendors weren't constantly updating, refining, and re-engineering to meet changing demands, products had a much longer shelf-life.

In the past, we pushed products and services; today demand *pulls* them through the value chain. The consumer wants a particular product or service when and where he wants it in real time. To stay in business today, marketers must have their product or service at the right place at the right time and at value pricing.

■ Consumer Demand Response

The proliferation of alternative channels of distribution have radically changed the way consumers/customers approach buying. Mass merchants, discounters, vendor outlets, and factory-direct selling have alerted consumers to customary markups in traditional distribution channels.

Indeed, "middleman" has become a dirty word in the consumer lexicon. Catalogs, direct mail, and the various forms of electronic commerce have given the consumer greater power. A telephone or an on-line computer and a credit card bring a world of products and services into the consumer's home in as little as 24 hours.

To satisfy heightened consumer expectations, marketers must apply *consumer demand response* (CDR) techniques to their supply chain management. Unfortunately, many traditional marketers are still working with creaky, bloated supply chains that are incapable of timely response to consumers' demands. They are still working on six- to eight-month business cycles that tie up capital in inventory that no one will need or want for months. Given the volatile nature of consumer demand, those products may be out-of-date by the time they reach the customer. With increased emphasis on value pricing and product or service on demand, how can consumer products companies, manufacturers, retailers, and service providers compete? How do they create a lean, mean, consumer-responsive supply chain?

They begin by taking their cues from the supermarket industry which pioneered consumer responsive distribution chains through concepts such as just-in-time (JIT) distribution and quick response (QR). Or they look to the examples set by J. C. Penney, Nordstrom's, Dillards, and Dayton-Hudson department store operations that have built profits based on distribution channels modeled on consumer demand response.

The first step toward an efficient distribution channel is to acknowledge and identify the problem. Consistently high inventory levels (equal to two or more months of sales), being regularly overstocked in out-of-season items, warehouses filled with products that are gathering dust, and generally stocking the wrong products at the wrong time are indications that a company is wasting money and losing sales due to a poorly managed supply chain. Failing to take advantage of the latest technology to deliver services efficiently and on time is another example of a badly managed distribution chain.

Once the problem is identified, the focus must shift from the supplier to the customer by monitoring and predicting consumer/customer demand. The responsibility falls to each member of the supply chain from retailer to the raw materials supplier.

JUMP START . . . .

1. Ask each member of your team to profile your company's customers, clients, or consumers. Does everyone agree?
2. Discuss how you can open up channels of communications with your customers/consumers.
3. Create and implement an action plan to improve customer/consumer communications.

■ Partnering and Communications Expedite Change

Communications is the catalyst that ensures a high-performance supply chain. In the past, communications was essentially a one-way street with information moving from suppliers of raw materials, to vendors, distributors, retailers, and finally consumers. In the case of a service provider, communications flowed from the vendor to the field staff to the customer or consumer. Today, effective supply channel management requires a multilane communications highway with emphasis on information moving backward through the chain from consumer to vendor.

Technology is hastening this shift in communications. Point-of-sale data captured on computers can communicate extensive information directly back to the distributor, the manufacturer, and the raw materials supplier providing important information that can shape the decisions of each member of the supply chain. Such information can help each link in the supply chain to stay in-stock on hot items and keep inventory low on less desired items. It can also give indications of future consumer demand.

For example, if consumers are snapping up super hot salsa at the supermarket and that information is fed back up the supply chain in a timely manner, the manufacturer is able to keep the hot salsa flowing through the supply chain and make more informed decisions about future product offerings. He can also transfer that information back to the chili pepper growers who can make better decisions on which varieties to plant the next season. Equally important, the salsa manufacturer isn't producing large quantities of the mild salsa that few consumers want. Similarly, an independent insurance agent using a laptop computer can communicate sales information back to the insurance company providing real time data that can help the company formulate its offerings. Each link in the supply chain cuts costs by eliminating unwanted products and services, while speeding up delivery of those that do meet consumer demand.

Getting information about your customer through the supply chain can tell you what your consumer/customer has already purchased. You also need to know what that customer is going to purchase in the future. Unless you're blessed with ESP, this can only be accomplished by knowing your customer inside and out. That *is* the new consumerism—getting inside your customer's head, understanding the dynamics of how the consumer thinks, then *listening and responding* to those needs.

■ The 80-20 Rule Still Rules

Many facets of U.S. business have reached maturation. There is no vast wave of neo-baby boomers to carry sales to new heights. Still, to succeed in the next millennium, companies must develop more customers and entice them to purchase products and services more frequently. The old 80-20 rule applies to service providers and business-to-business vendors as well as retailers and manufacturers. You must learn more about those 20 percent of your customers who buy 80 percent of your goods and services and cater to them.

To do that, you first have to know who your customer is today and who that customer could be tomorrow. You have to know how to prioritize your customers, where they are, and how to reach them.

Where do you start? Begin with your company's consumer history and move forward. Start with whatever data you have gathered in the past, even if it's nothing more than a mailing list. Then begin building a consumer database that will help you satisfy your customers' needs and give you an opportunity to "go back to the future" in terms of service. In the 1950s and 1960s, we knew our customers better. We did a better job of listening and responding. Today computer sales readouts have frequently replaced face-to-face contact with customers. We have to use that computer technology to learn more about our customers. We can listen and respond using the following techniques:

- *Surveys* provide broad samples of answers to targeted questions.

- *Psychographics* tell us more about the values and lifestyles of the many different types of customers that are out there.

- *Consumer panels* involve inviting customers to your place of business to get a more quantitative feeling for their likes and dislikes and a sense of how to better service them.

- *Customer jamborees* offer products in a small, personal group setting that allows for good consumer feedback on products and services.

- *Suggestion boxes at point of sale* and *comment cards* allow an open door for a constant flow of information from consumers who buy your products or services.

- *Focus groups* are particularly good for mid- and large-sized businesses that want to be more in tune with their consumers, improve their products and services, and assess where they are in relation to their competition.

- *Mall and store intercepts* give input from a broader geographic and wider economic profile.

- *800 numbers* maintain an open door for customer service accessibility and improve understanding of customer needs and wants.

- *Chat lines* that appear on-line on computers allow companies to reach out to consumers who are beyond a company's immediate geographic boundaries.

- *Market research* provides quantitative feedback and an objective, nonemotional understanding of the market for which a company is positioning itself.

These technology-driven marketing tools offer ways to both *listen* and *respond*. Your consumer can, for example, call you on an 800 number, and you, in turn, can *listen* and *respond*. Chat lines, mall and store intercepts, and focus groups also offer two-way communications.

Once you start listening and responding, customers will keep coming back for proprietary reasons, because you are addressing their needs. In addition, listening and responding give you value-added ideas and help sustain your competitive advantage.

As communication flows in, you will analyze this information to create a unique position for your company and offer your customers the goods or services they are requesting. From that unique positioning, two things begin to happen.

1. You start to increase customer frequency because you are responding and listening. Customers come back because you are addressing their needs.
2. As you maintain customer frequency, your company grows and attains its gross margin goals. Just as important, your New Consumerism approach will give your firm a more positive, consumer-driven image.

When you respond to your consumers, opportunities open up—new markets, new customers, and new lifestyle trends. Consumer communication can uncover particle markets—those smaller, demassed particles of larger markets such as Chicago's affluent Mexican-American market, communities of Vietnamese immigrants in California, and literary groups in small towns. Each offers the right marketer an opportunity. As you discover these pockets of consumers with their individual regionalisms, ethnicities, and special interests, you will be able to better tailor your marketing programs and maximize profits. These and other markets can, for the first time, become part of your customer mix. New, evolving customer segments such as OPALS (Older People with Active Lifestyles), Generation X-ers, graying baby boomers, zoomers (boomers in their thirties), and even the Echo and Millennium Generations can open up to you.

■ Knowledge Is Power

Knowledge has always been power, but in the Information Age, knowledge is essential. Technology will allow us to know customers better than ever. Databasing, an essential information tool for cataloguers, will be important to all marketers from consumer products companies to business-to-business service providers. Computers will allow companies to save and retrieve vast stores of customer information. Along with basic customer information, databases will save information concerning customer demographics, previous purchases, sizes, color preferences, and other information that can aid in marketing more effectively to existing customers. Marketers will go *datamining* in their databases looking for nuggets of information that can direct future marketing efforts. Databases will provide us with *market basket* information—what products are frequently purchased together. For example, just as bacon and eggs are frequently found in the same market basket at the supermarket, sports-specific athletic shoes and socks or pocket recordings and recording tapes are frequently sold together. By analyzing databases, we will be able to develop more sophisticated market basket information.

Technology will also provide us with virtual reality environments. A driver training school will be able to give students a feel for the road before they ever get behind the wheel. A sporting goods retailer will offer customers an opportunity to practice their drives on a simulated eighteenth hole, right in the store. Store personnel will refer to their *smart wallets* and hand-held computers that provide complete customer information instantaneously. Billing information, sizes, customer's preferred sports, and previous purchases will all be available on the smart wallet. Technology will enable businesses to have the necessary information to respond to customer demand as we move into the 21st century.

Think of your business as a wheel, such as the one shown in Exhibit 10–1, with consumerism as the axle. For a consumer products company, a manufacturer or service provider, purchasing, operations, merchandising, distribution, and strategic marketing/consumer marketing, along with information systems, form the spokes supporting the business wheel. Information and the systems we install to deliver that information is just one spoke in the wheel driving your business.

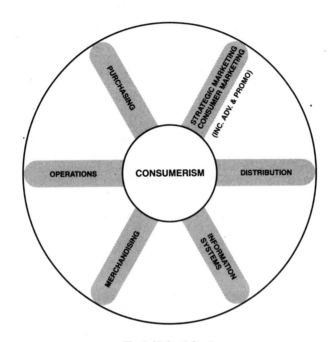

Exhibit 10–1
Consumer Products Company/Manufacturer/
Service Provider

Consumerism is also the axle of the retailer's business wheel as in Exhibit 10–2. Here, product and merchandising, operations, manufacturing and sourcing, strategic marketing/consumer marketing, distribution and information systems are the spokes that support the business wheel.

No matter who or what you sell, you must subscribe to the New Consumerism and know your customer. Today's consumers and customers have many choices; you must make them see your product or service as having a reason for being or your store as a destination. Making the customer king or queen and installing him or her as your CEO is a good place to start.

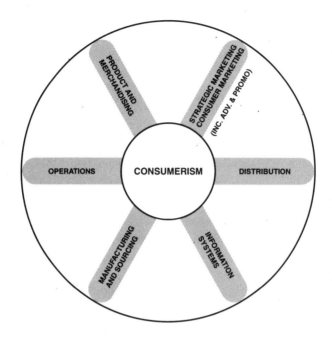

Exhibit 10-2
Consumerism Chart—Retail

JUMP START . . . .

To begin your databasing program:

1. Discuss what information databasing can provide and what your team believes it needs to learn about you customers or consumers.

2. Determine what techniques you can use to gather data, such as surveys, comment cards, and mall intercepts.

3. Work with your information systems department to implement a databasing program.

11

The New Marketing

Information, Information, Information!

The world is but a school of inquiry.

Michel de Montaigne, French essayist

With the development of the New Consumerism, the role of marketing has grown and evolved. Your marketing department is "ground zero" for ongoing strategic planning and provides continuous information links to all segments of your company. As a critical link in the Strategic Value Chain, it relates closely to sales, products or services, and technology.

Does your marketing department mirror that evolution? Or does it still function as most did ten years ago when marketing activities were typically limited to advertising, promotion, public relations, and a bit of market research? Back then information flowed one way—*out* from marketing to the consumer, the customer, and the various middlemen. Advertising, promotion, and public relations told the company's story. Unfortunately, they didn't always tell the same story or project the same image.

Does that describe your marketing function today? Or is your marketing department a conduit for multiple flows of information? Does information constantly flow *in* from consumers, customers, and all the links across the Strategic Value Chain? Does your marketing department's databasing function and other methodologies provide a continuous informational flow out to key departments such as sales, production, and technology? Does input and reaction from those departments then flow back to the marketing department?

To work effectively, your marketing department should embrace six major activities:

1. Strategic planning.
2. Databasing.
3. Research.
4. Advertising.
5. Promotion.
6. Benchmarking and best practices.

Within this network of activities, *integrated marketing* is a key buzzword. Remember the exercise in which each of your executives described a lemon? Put that exercise to work to be certain every activity of your marketing department is communicated with the same message and the same image. Is your advertising, promotion, and research dictated by the vision, mission, and strategic goals of your company? Are each of these activities *intermarketing related?* Are they organized to work toward the same goals, image, and knowledge or are they moving in independent directions?

■ **Databasing: Foundation for Strategic Planning**

Through the strategic planning process your company is searching for its future—which begins tomorrow. Databasing, the accumulation of information from and about your consumer or customer, is vital to that process. Without this constant flow of consumer/customer information, you cannot make intelligent strategic planning decisions nor can your people understand the voids in the marketplace. Do you have a databasing system in place to provide the information you need to develop new products, services, and niches of opportunity for your current and future mix of consumers/customers?

Databasing provides *objective* information that is essential to help achieve the mission that you and your team are working toward. It also suggests new objectives for your company and provides new perspectives on current objectives. As your marketing department gathers information, it must be shared with other departments to get their input. Thus the continuous flow of information keeps your company in perpetual motion.

Do the other departments in your company see marketing as a strategic link for information that will help them think through their ideas and get a clearer picture of what's happening in the marketplace? Is marketing providing the information that can turn ideas into reality effectively and efficiently?

■ Knowledge Is Power: Share the Power

Top management is responsible for creating an environment in which each department openly shares information. Is information shared freely within your organization, or do department heads jealously guard their information? The technology department, for example, traditionally believed it held power because it controlled information. But to compete in today's marketplace, all departments must recognize that power must be shared. When even one link in the Strategic Value Chain closes off to another, all strategic links are crippled.

JUMP START . . . .

---

1. Ask each team member how he or she views the current role of the marketing department.

2. Assess the kind of information each department currently receives from marketing and how to improve the level of information.

3. Discuss how the flow of information in and out of marketing can be improved.

■ **From Product "Gap" to Individual Preferences**

Has your marketing department moved beyond simply identifying and exploring avenues of opportunities such as "gaps" for a product, a service, or product advantages to focusing on target audiences, individual customer preferences, consumer demographics, and lifestyles? Today, marketers are striving to improve marketing performance by targeting products and services to particular market niches (i.e., the many ethnic markets). Are you emphasizing customer service and loyalty programs as tools to strengthen and sustain your customer relationships in today's crowded and competitive marketplace? Are you "de-massing" your marketing efforts in an attempt to achieve sales and profit goals more effectively and efficiently?

A key to better marketing is to focus your entire company on your customer. Use computerized marketing technology to track relationships with your consumer/customer—facilitating easier order taking and making certain the right products and services get to the right place at the right time.

■ High-Tech Intimacy

Do you see computers as instruments of depersonalization? On the contrary, computer technology allows your company to become more intimate with your customers. To properly manage customer intimacy and find opportunities in the *New Marketing,* you must know both the methodology and economics of database marketing, which can provide valuable strategic information. In order to develop intimacy with their customers, all types of companies are adopting the database marketing skills that catalog companies have mastered. This information-driven marketing process can enable your company to:

- Develop, test, implement, measure, and appropriately modify customized marketing programs and strategies.
- Creatively act on emerging marketing opportunities to develop individual customer relationships and to further build business.
- Build traffic through direct marketing and identify the most efficient ways to generate leads and sales across the multiple communications and distribution channels.

Exchanging information with your customer is as important as the actual sale of your product or service. In some cases, companies are establishing on-going dialogues making use of in-package surveys, traditional surveys, focus groups, and other information-gathering techniques. Point-of-sale programs that automatically reward buyers with discounts and special offers while electronically recording what they are purchasing are another option.

Through dialogues you can gather information of *added value* to both your company and your customer, while enabling your customers to continually express their perceptions and attitudes about your products and services. Your marketing department can use this information to develop customized marketing strategies and programs for individuals or small groups of customers. You no longer have to settle for one single solution or program to fit complex marketing situations.

Significantly, if you can integrate individual customer information on a continuing basis, you can accurately and quickly evaluate your opportunities and more precisely identify who is buying what, how often, and why. Then link this information to those elements in the marketing mix that are most likely to motivate consumers to stay with your brand or service or switch to it.

The more you learn about your customers, the more you will realize they are not all alike. Your marketing department will continue to datamine, maintain, and analyze detailed information and relational data about customers and prospects, identifying key elements of the de-massed customer mix. You will also optimize the process of planning, pricing, and promoting, as well as closing a sale that satisfies both you and your customer.

■ How Technology Changes the 4 P's

Technology changes everything, including each of the 4 P's—Product, Price, Promotion, and Place. Before companies were able to take advantage of the consumer/customer information that technology provides, they had little basis for tailoring products and services to smaller customer segments. As a result, products and services were basically standard, as were the prices charged for them. With standard products and prices, one-size-fits-all promotions—typically national advertising, co-op advertising, and retailer coupons—were the norm.

Before technology changed marketing channels, most products were sold through traditional retail outlets, such as department stores, specialty shops, mass merchants, and catalogs. The 4 P's looked like the left side of Exhibit 11–1 with standard products, uniform promotions, fixed prices, and distribution (place) through general retail outlets.

As we cross the technology gap, moving toward the year 2000, the customer, rather than the market, becomes the center of the 4 P's, which are segmented to meet the changing and varying needs of the customer.

- *Product* (Exhibit 11–2) today is variable, rather than standard, with companies offering increasing varieties of products and services designed to fit the many consumer/customer needs. Technology is providing the customer information companies need to effectively adapt their products and services to variable needs and wants in "real time."

- *Place* (Exhibit 11–3) now includes a growing number of alternative channels of distribution. Technology has created home shopping, interactive TV, 800 numbers,

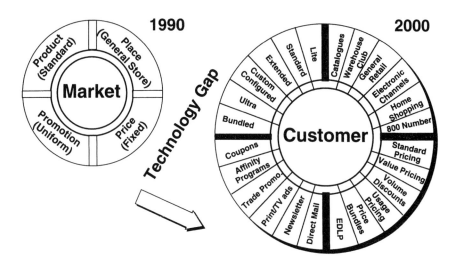

Exhibit 11–1
The New 4 P's

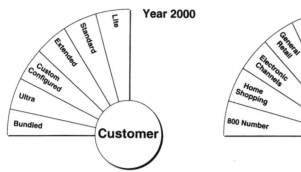

Exhibit 11–2
Product (Variable)

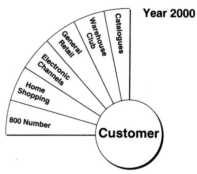

Exhibit 11–3
Place (Alternative Channel)

and electronic channels, such as the Internet and CD-Rom. Technology is also behind the growth of catalogs, allowing mail order marketers to hone their product expertise and their service.

• *Price* (Exhibit 11–4). Technology provides the customer information needed to tailor prices to create strong demand. Today we see every day low prices (EDLP), price bundles, usage pricing, and volume discounts. Now, with bar coding technology, changing prices is as fast and easy as the touch of a key stroke.

Exhibit 11–4
Price (Variable)

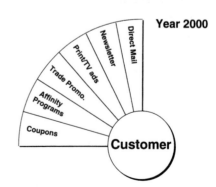

Exhibit 11–5
Promotion (Multi)

- *Promotion* (Exhibit 11–5) Technology is the driver for a new world of promotion. Now companies can pinpoint direct mail to market segments and particles. They can even personalize their message with the customer's name. Coupons are now more effectively directed to those who are most likely to use them. Both printed and electronic newsletters, maintained on a company's Web site, can bring a company's message to its customers. Affinity programs, such as Delta's or American Airline's frequent flyer clubs, not only reward customers for, but also help build brand loyalty and allows the airlines to track the travel patterns of their best customers.

Technology, as an enabler, allows more accurate and faster tracking of information to and from the customer and throughout the entire value chain. Technology has changed the 4 P's and it is changing everything else as we will discuss in Chapter 14 and in Part V.

■ Segmentation Is the Key to Success!

The bank ATM machine is a prime example of service companies using information to segment markets and reach consumers with the right product at the right time. Banks gather data at point-of-sale both through the ATM machine itself and telephones located at ATM sites. Banks have used this continuous flow of information to tailor and refine their offerings. Five years ago, the ATM machine was essentially a tool to provide customers with access to cash on a 24-hour basis. Today, the consumer can make deposits, retrieve information on account balances, review which checks have cleared, and transfer money from one account to another. In areas with strong ethnic markets, customers can conduct their business in Spanish, Chinese, Arabic, and other languages. Banks have further extended services by allowing customers to pay bills and take out loans on-line. All of these developments are in response to information the consumer has provided at point-of-sale.

The ATM is just one illustration of how the inflow of information allows companies to reach consumers with the right product at the right time. Information can help your company achieve other strategic goals. It can:

- Help formulate new strategies.
- Drive new programs and fuel new revenue sources.
- Foster new services and generate repeat orders, prompting consumers to buy more products with more frequency. For examples, magazines promote gift subscription renewals by sending donors lists of those people to whom they sent gift subscriptions in the previous year.
- Increase your customer loyalty. Communications helps your company take advantage of the 80/20 rule by pinpointing the 20 percent of the customers who do buy 80 percent of products or services. Information provides an opportunity to concentrate attention on those prime buyers and closely examine their needs and wants. Customer loyalty programs, for example, are usually targeted to the most active 20 percent of the company's database. Companies are also finding success in targeting promotions and bonus offers based on previous purchases, buying patterns, and consumer/customers preferences.

Your company will garner the greatest benefit from the New Marketing if you continuously gather, store, and use such information to your competitive advantage by developing new strategies that carefully target programs. Managing the communications mix and developing different customer contact strategies for different types of customers is also important. Today you can achieve this with more precision than ever before by:

- Analyzing relevant and timely customer information.
- Correlating customer-level data with traditional measures of off-the-shelf purchases.
- Creating on-going customers dialogues to funnel relevant information to the marketing database.
- Enhancing databases with surveys, demographics, psychographics, and lifestyle data.
- Identifying who is buying what and how often.

In addition to functioning as a conduit of information, your marketing department must help induce customers to buy your products or services by creating an image and awareness of your company and by promoting your unique competitive advantage. Marketing can, for example, convey the message that a company is a unique store (such as The Home Depot or Bed, Bath and Beyond), that it offers a unique product/service (such as Levi's computerized custom fit jeans), or that it provides a unique service (such as Federal Express's new software package that allows customers to order pickups and deliveries on-line).

Activities that support this aspect of your marketing department's responsibilities may include direct marketing (which is, in fact, synonymous with databasing), telemarketing, planning of media and advertising, and planning and execution of promotional events and promotions. With the growing focus on information gathering, your marketing department must not lose its edge in getting information back to the client, customer, or consumer. Again, all these functions must be tied to the vision, mission, and objectives and be intermarketing related.

Finally, you will want to incorporate *benchmarking* and *best practices* as means of tracking and comparing your business capabilities with those of other companies in your industry and in others. Benchmarking is the process of assessing and measuring data such as a company's operational results, by comparing them with the results of other companies. Since such information may be difficult to find, create a reference library adding information as you find it. Think of this as a databasing function.

Through best practices you gain an understanding of how you company compares with others in your industry in terms of cost of doing business, the success or failure of products or services, the breakout of different processes and costs, distribution and logistics, and other information. Industry information may be available through associations, annual reports, and research companies. Analyze and compare the data to see where your company fits, then integrate what you have learned into the New Marketing.

The New Marketing is an essential link in the Strategic Value Chain. Without the vital information from marketing, any attempt at product and service assessments or sales assessments would be futile. In the old days, companies simply designed their products and services and sent them out to the marketplace. Today, they must be created to fit the needs of the customer and the demands of the marketplace. Armed with what you know now, let's move on and look at how well your products and services fit.

JUMP START . . . .

To assess the information going out from marketing to your consumers and customers:

1. Gather and review all advertising—consumer and trade—and all promotional materials.
2. Discuss how these materials and the media or environment in which they appear support the mission and objectives of the company.
3. Discuss whether these materials are intermarketing related. Do they send a consistent image and message?

12

Does the Product or Service Still Fit?

I don't know the key to success, but the key to failure is trying to please everybody.

Bill Cosby, American actor and author

Products or services tend to be the focal point of a marketing strategy. But how do your current products or services fit with your new vision, mission, and objectives? How does the consumer/customer information that is flowing into your marketing department via databasing, research, and other techniques match with the products or services you are selling? Are you really offering the products or services that your customers say they need?

Product/service assessment is vital as both a link in the Strategic Value Chain and an on-going company function. During the assessment, you will seek to answer the following:

- Which of your products or services could more customers buy more frequently?

- What are your customers telling you that could lead to product or service improvements or developments that could be an extension of your business?
- Based on what you are learning about consumer demand, what new products and services could you create?

Product/service assessment can be broken into three pieces:

1. *Assessment and improvement of current products and services.* Information coming back through the supply chain or market research data may show a product or service is becoming marginal and no longer fits with current consumer needs. Should you phase out the product or service or make changes that would update and revive it?

2. *Consideration of new products or services based on consumer/customer input.* For example, a cosmetic company could analyze information provided by survey cards included in product packaging and discover growing consumer preference for products that contain sun blocks. Using this information, the company can consider creating a new group of products by adding sunblock to its foundations or moisturizers. In the same way, a veterinarian who maintains a chat line could learn that consumers are interested in preventive care for their pets. The vet might then institute a series of low cost preventive care seminars, such as "How to help your pet thrive in the winter months."

3. *Exploration of new products or services, which market research indicates would fulfill consumer needs, but which are based on new technology the consumer isn't aware of.* Windows 95 enjoyed what may be the biggest product launch of all times. Microsoft's new system was ahead of the vast majority of its customers. The product offered software features most Microsoft customers didn't know existed. But Microsoft knows its customers well enough to say, "If we build it, they will come."

In assessing new products and services, first learn the extent of demand, then think about price and other factors. Remember too that products and services should be evolutionary, not revolutionary! A new product or service must be related to and rooted in your current offerings. Don't start thinking about manufacturing television sets, if your expertise and reputation is built on lawn furniture. Don't go into the catering business if your expertise is in beauty care. Then ask yourself: Where can we make or source these products? What quality features do we need to offer in our new service? How can we make these products or services value added in terms of price?

■ Product/Service Links to Success

Are you offering a service such as America Online's on-line information or Jenny Craig's weight loss program. Are you selling a product such as the *New York Times,* Jello gelatin, or a Ford Taurus? Each of these products and services has very specific attributes which sets it apart from competing products and services. Understanding and capitalizing on these differences is essential in building a brand.

What are the attributes of your products in terms of quality, style, brand, packaging, color, or price? What are the attributes of your service in terms of reliability, timeliness, or exclusivity? What are the benefits of your product or service? Consider both the tangibles and intangibles. Does it genuinely have added value? Does it provoke an image of sex, such as many jeans brands do? If you offer a food product, does it say "diet" or "lite"? Does it suggest fitness and health or indulgence? Does your service make any statement which the buyer accepts as offering want-satisfaction?

Remember that a product or a service is not a commodity. It's a bundle of perceptions based on packaging, advertising, promotion, past performance, and hundreds of other pieces of information that the customer "knows" about the product. A smart company sells value and benefits, not just products or services.

Consider your perceptions about the following lists of products and services:

Guess jeans	Wrangler jeans
Ben and Jerry's ice cream	Sealtest ice cream
Dole pineapple	Foodtown pineapple
Arm & Hammer baking soda	everyone else's baking soda
Federal Express	Ace Delivery Service
Vidal Sassoon	Sally's Cut and Curl
Lawn Boy	The kid who mows your lawn

Remember that one product or service is never interchangeable with another. The consumer has feelings and attitudes toward branded goods based on their experiences in the marketplace. Be very aware of what your products or services really mean to your customers.

■ What Constitutes a New Product or Service?

When is a product or service truly new and when is it just a modification on an old product?

- *A product or service is new if it is innovative and truly unique.* Digital dishes, the first plain paper fax, the WonderBra, and AT&T's ISDN direct access to the Internet are all innovative products. The Home Shopping Network also broke new ground as the first interactive television shopping service. Each was unique in the marketplace when it was introduced. All those which followed were imitations or adaptations.

- *A product or service may also be considered new if it is a replacement for an existing product and is significantly different from existing ones.* The Gillette razor for women, slim slips and other "shape" clothing, and wrinkle-free cotton are examples. Similarly, MCI and Sprint introduced discounted long distance telephone service. Each of these offered a significant improvement over previous products. Their benefits were unique to the marketplace.

- *An imitative product or service can also be considered new if it is new to your company, but not to the marketplace.* Examples include the host of intimate apparel manufacturers producing WonderBra knockoffs or additional producers of plain paper faxes, digital dishes, and on-line services. Most product and service introductions fall into this category. The key to a successful launch of an imitator is to create a product which offers a unique bundle of benefits and added value. You have to give the customer a reason to buy your product.

During the planning and development process you must answer these questions:

- Which product or service should the company make?
- Should the company market more or fewer products or services?
- What new uses are there for each product or service?
- What brand label and package should be used for each product?
- How should the product be designed and packaged and in what sizes and colors should it be produced?
- In what quantities should it be produced? Should it be marketed regionally, nationally, or globally?
- How should the product or service be priced? How does price add value?
- How does this product or service tie back to our vision, mission, objectives, and the other strategic links?

JUMP START . . . .

To review your current products or services:

1. Discuss which of your products or services could be sold to more customers and which you could sell more of to existing customers.

2. Discuss what stage of their life cycle your products and services are in. Are they nearing retirement or can they be improved or adapted for greater sales?

3. Discuss whether complementary products and services can be added to extend your current line.

■ Core Product/Service or Passing Fancy?

In assessing your products and services, ask which of your products or services are core competencies on which your business is based and which are embellishments? Consider the basic five-pocket jean, a core competency for any jeans or bottoms maker. The jean in blue denim or black with flared or pegged legs is a core competency. Add fashion colors such as lavender, kelly green, or fuchsia or embellish it with embroidery, patches, or studs and you've moved beyond the core product. Those lavender jeans may make a million one season, but they'll be dead the next.

Service businesses also have core offerings. For a veterinarian, annual shots and checkups are core competencies, while services such as teeth cleaning and grooming are not. To survive, a company must nurture its core competencies, those products or services that sell year after year.

■ Cradle to Grave

As you assess your products or services, remember that they, like people, have a life cycle. A product or service's stage in that life cycle will dictate how much attention and nurturing it will demand. In *infancy*, products and services need careful nurturing. A name must be chosen, along with price, packaging, distribution, and promotion programs. The product or service must be properly introduced to the market. During this stage, the new offering will probably have a negative cash flow.

As the product or service becomes acclimated to the marketplace, it will enter its *growth* stage. Now it will expand its territory and venture into new markets. Advertising may be instituted to build demand among consumers. During this stage, a product or service shows its true potential, but may still just break even.

During *maturity*, the product or service reaches its full potential. If it has been nurtured properly, it becomes a *cash cow*, requiring less financial investment. During this time, the company may begin to consider new versions of the product or service. New technology may be incorporated or new uses may be found.

During the fourth stage, *old age*, sales begin to fade. The company must decide whether to retire their product or service or adapt it to fit new consumer requirements. Those products that no longer meet the company's strategic objectives may be retired early.

While key brands such as Kleenex tissues and Arm & Hammer baking soda enjoy a very long maturity, others, such as the Pet Rock, are fads that move through the life cycle quickly. Since no product or service lives forever, new introductions are essential. To survive and grow, a company must add new products and services. In introducing these, a number of factors can work to both support and impede new product or service development. Consider these:

- Technology.
- Changing consumer needs.
- Globalization, international competition in new markets.
- Government regulations.
- High or low cost of capital.
- High or low cost of labor.
- Changes in consumer values, e.g., conspicuous to non-conspicuous consumption.
- Added value.

Products and services are essential strategic links. They play a major role in the execution of a strategic market plan. For example, does your company want to defend a market share position? Then increase market share by introducing an addition to an existing product line or revising an existing service. Does your company want to further its reputation as an innovator? Then introduce a really new product or service, not just an extension of an existing one.

But first, be sure that the product or service links with the company's present marketing structure. Can present channels of distribution be used? Can the existing salesforce be used? Does the product or service tie into the mission and vision of the company? Since these assessments will be conducted by your strategic assessment team, you will know how the company's divisions view the various aspects of the product or service. By so empowering your team, you will decrease reluctance to change, increase authority, and give your new product or service the best chance for success.

Throughout history, all successful launches have had at least one of three advantages: a product or service advantage (the Volkswagen Beetle or America Online), a marketing advantage (Avon Cosmetics door-to-door marketing approach), or a creative advertising advantage (Avis's We're No. 2 campaign). A successful launch is also grounded in customer knowledge. Your motto for product or service assessment could be: "Know thy customer; know thy product or service."

JUMP START . . . .

Consider new products or services:

1. Discuss what new products or services you should be considering to stay competitive.
2. Discuss how those products or services would further your mission and objectives.
3. Assess how these products or services would fit with your current sales, production, and competitive space. Assess the costs of bringing these new products or services to market.

13

Channel Power

The Big Sell

It is only shallow people who do not judge by appearances.

Oscar Wilde, *The Picture of Dorian Gray*

Using the LINKS process, you've looked at new opportunities. You've analyzed your research and listened to your consumers and customers to learn what they want. You've used this information to assess your products and services. So how are you going to sell those products and services? How does your current sales structure fit into the vision, mission, and objectives? Now you must ask yourself: Where can we sell it? How can we sell it? How can we sell it effectively? Since your products or services are the direct results of consumer/customer feedback, the old protest, "But, we really can't sell that." doesn't hold. You may not be able to sell product X or service Y using the old channels of distribution or traditional sales methods. So your strategic assessment team's task in examining the sales link is to find the distribution channels and the sales structure that can best bring your products or services to your customers.

For example, new distribution capabilities are opening up in the field of electronic commerce with new, developing applications such as the Internet, CD-ROM, wireless communication, or virtual reality. Are your current customers utilizing those new areas of distribution? Are there potential customers you could reach or existing customers that you could sell more to through those channels of distribution? If they are out there, who are they? And what do they need? What will it take from all of your resources to give them what they need?

You have introduced the New Consumerism to your company. You understand who your current consumers are and who you want to reach in the future. So how and where do you reach those customers? What new and changing avenues of distribution do you need to look at? There are three steps in this stage of the sales assessment.

1. *Look at your current avenues of distribution.* Are they shrinking or growing and why? For example, consumers have become disenchanted with department stores' high prices and lack of service. As a result, department store share of market has been shrinking steadily over the past 15 plus years, while the big boxes and other discounters have grown. How much of your product is sold through a shrinking avenue of distribution and what does that say about your future sales potential? Examine your company's market share and your industry's market share to determine which current distribution markets are growing. If you are in the home improvement business and consumers are shopping discounters, you can't reach those markets unless you are selling retailers such as Lowes and The Home Depot. If you are selling a business service and have been relying on trade shows to reach your customers, has attendance been off lately? Then it's time to look for other channels.

2. *Look at new avenues of distribution* such as electronic commerce which offers marketplaces without boundaries. Can you reach current and new customers through one or more forms of electronic commerce? Then decide how you can sell through these new and growing channels of distribution.

3. *Decide what image and position you need to partici-pate in the new marketplaces.* If you are a kingpin in a re-ceding market, how do you maintain that competitive edge? Or if your market is eroding, is it time to take some of your eggs out of that basket? In which markets can you spread out those eggs and reach new consumers?

Once you've found the right markets, you must learn the needs of those distribution channels. For example, if you market home improvement products or services and decide that your offerings should be sold in outlets such as The Home Depot, you must ask:

- Do you and can you fit into their program?
- Can you give the markup structure they need? And how can you re-engineer to achieve their markup structure?
- How can you capitalize on retail space within the given environment? For example, should you look at special fixturing or packaging that provides comprehensive point-of-sale information?
- What is your competitive edge against your competi-tion in that area of distribution?
- What type of marketing communications package can you develop to reach that consumer and how can it be integrated into that environment in terms of point-of-sale?
- If those marketplaces are saturated with other prod-ucts or services, what new markets can you look at? What alternative marketplaces can you move into, such as electronic commerce, going global, or moving to the next town.

Once you have established *where* you think you can sell, the question becomes: *How* are you going to sell it? How can technology help you facilitate the sale? What is the most cost efficient methodology?

- Will you sell direct and by what means? Telemarketing sales, door-to-door, or through company outlets?
- Will you employ sales representatives?
- Will you use in-house account executives?
- Will you sell electronically on the Internet?

Consider also the communications tools you will need. Do you want your sales people to present your program on CD-ROM? If so, they will need computers to make their presentation. What other tools do they need to communicate? Are those tools integrated in terms of the message, image, and position you are trying express? Considering each of these interlinking variables is the basis of the Strategic Value Chain in which each link works with the next to build synergistically.

Examining how your sales people communicate your message and whether they are communicating in the most effective manner is important. Equally important—what is your competition doing, or not doing, that *you* could be doing to help close the sale? This is true for service providers as well as manufacturers and consumer products companies. For example, travel agencies specializing in business accounts may ensure better service by providing their major customers with on-site agents. Or a local sandwich shop may create a competitive advantage by accepting lunch orders by fax.

Be aware of the blurring of lines between one channel of distribution and others. Until recently, vendors chose a limited number of distribution channels. An upscale product such as quality home furnishings would have been sold through department or specialty stores. Today, such products might also be sold in factory direct outlets, in on-line catalogues, CD-ROMs, or infomercials.

With the new electronic revolution, the rules are continually evolving. We are doing business without bricks and mortar as selling loses its boundaries and becomes global. Consolidation and technology are driving these changes and, through it all, the consumer is taking greater control.

Traditional retailing through department, specialty, and discount stores is being challenged by non-store retailing. Party plans, door-to-door selling, automatic vending machines and kiosks, selling on trucks, electronic retailing, hypermarkets, and mail order are all legitimate avenues today. Using multiple marketing channels is a strategic alternative as shown in Exhibit 13–1. The tire manufacturer in this illustration has developed six separate channels to bring the product to the end user.

A service provider also has many more channels available. An information service company, for example, might

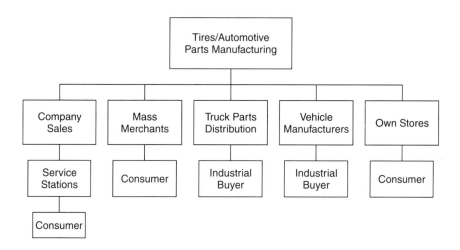

Exhibit 13–1
Channel Power—Manufacturer

once have marketed their information through a newsletter or publication. Today, they might also market and deliver their service over the Internet and other channels as shown in Exhibit 13–2.

That is *channel power* in action. Today's marketers must create power bases for developing channel leadership by systematically planning and evaluating distribution as a controllable variable. Today distribution decisions are part of all phases of the strategic planning process. They must be evaluated continually.

■ Interactive Selling in the 21st Century

Over the next 15 years, advances in communications and information technology will radically change the process of

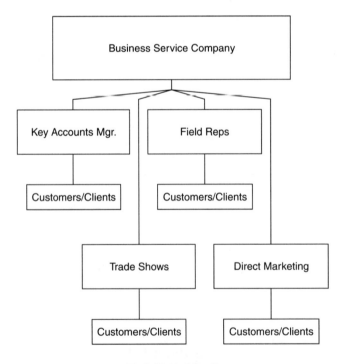

Exhibit 13–2
Channel Power—Service Provider

selling and buying. Whether it's an outside salesperson making a presentation to a buyer, a telemarketer speaking with a customer, a retail clerk influencing a shopper, or a consumer gathering information electronically from a television set, personal computer, or a kiosk, the sales process will become more efficient, more effective, and faster. Interactive selling tools and other sales improvement tools are being integrated with the use of laptop computers, CD-ROMs, multimedia presentation tools, and high-speed data communications networks. It is now possible for a salesforce to carry around vast amounts of sales and marketing information that provide customers with answers they need to make a buying decision. Such interactive selling systems represent a significant opportunity to substantially improve corporate revenues and profits. The application of information technology to the selling process is quickly evolving from a strategic advantage to a strategic necessity!

Where do you begin? By mapping out both the sales and customer buying processes. From those vantage points, you can link computer and communications technologies to the business goals that mesh your vision into your strategic marketing plan. This is often a difficult task, because companies are frequently boxed in by traditional sales channels.

The selling process in most companies is as old as the company itself. These companies need to seriously apply "thinking out of the box" processes to their sales efforts. Managers often have difficulty accurately defining the steps that comprise the sales process. In the wake of strong customer demands, addressing this area becomes imperative, particularly in the face of growing global competition.

Even in this new age of selling, the traditional principles of selling remain. The sales person must still follow the four stages of the sales process:

1. *Prospecting*—Seeking out potential customers.
2. *Qualifying*—Determining whether the customer is viable.

3. *Developing*—Providing information that allows the customer to make a decision.

4. *Closing*—Getting the customer or consumer to commit.

Even with the latest technology, the salesperson must still:

- Plan strategies for their region.
- Execute their plans.
- Control the progress of their plans.

Fortunately, the new technological tools and freedom to explore the many, growing distribution channels make the selling process far more exciting and challenging than ever before.

JUMP START . . .

For each of your products or services:

1. Assess current channels of distribution. Are they growing or shrinking? Are they profitable?

2. Discuss where you believe your customers and potential customers can be found.

3. Assess possible new avenues of distribution. Are they consistent with your vision, mission and objectives?

4. How must your company position itself to participate in these marketplaces?

14

Real Time

Any sufficiently advanced technology is indistinguishable from magic.

Arthur C. Clarke, *The Lost Worlds of 2001*

The type of business your company engages in, your corporate culture, and your competitive environment provide both opportunities and restrictions. The freedom to make decisions based on internal and external marketing factors is vital to your survival in today's marketplace. Technology offers that freedom. It is key to maintaining flexibility, responsiveness to change, speed to marketplace, and reducing overhead.

In addition to being an enabler for all these critical functions, technology is a tool to interact with and to help find new approaches for accomplishing tasks. It also allows business to be boundary-less, reaching beyond its geographical limits through electronic commerce.

Firms must become more involved in the innovation process. They must be prepared to exploit new opportunities as they evolve and examine how those opportunities could help develop innovation, speed to market, better analyses, and future scenarios.

Every area of your business is affected by technology. Training and development departments, for example, are taking training out of the classroom with the use of CD-ROMs, video, teleconferencing, and on-line computing to deliver educational programs.

Bar coding technology is allowing companies to re-engineer their physical distribution, speeding products to market, cutting operating costs and providing real time information. Now restaurants, including the white tablecloth establishments, are using technology to speed orders and checks. Waiters are equipped with handheld computers that automatically flash your order directly to the kitchen and later send that information on to the cashier.

Computer technology is changing the way salespeople interact with their customers, allowing them to sell better and smarter. It allows for interactive selling and creates new channels for reaching the consumer.

Technology is enabling the creation of new products and changing the way those products are manufactured. E-mail, Lotus notes, and fax-mail are changing the way everyone within the organization and outside of it communicates with one another and performs tasks.

Ongoing developments in technology affect each of the strategic links and is discussed within each chapter. How is technology changing the way you do business? If you are keeping up-to-date, you know that technology is changing everything.

JUMP START . . . .

1. Ask each of your team members to investigate and then report on the latest technologies that could affect or improve his or her department.

2. Discuss how new technologies such as e-mail, teleconferencing, LANs, and on-line computing could change your company and open new opportunities.

3. Have your team assess intrabusiness benefits across the Strategic Value Chain vs. the investment of adopting new technologies.

15

Getting It to the Right Place at the Right Time

Time is money.

Benjamin Franklin, *Advice to a Young Tradesman*

Is your physical distribution geared up for the demands of the 21st century or would your warehousing operation be more appropriate as a setting for a Dickens novel? Can your operation meet the needs of real time, just-in-time, and quick response programs? Is your traffic department up to date or are your inbound transportation costs in chaos?

Physical distribution or logistics is concerned with transportation, storage, material handling, inventory control, distribution-related communications, and data processing. With the advent of warehouse automation and the growing demands of the marketplace, distribution is becoming an increasingly important strategic link.

Having established your marketing opportunities and marketing channels in the strategic process, you must next identify and design physical distribution systems to make sure the products are available. Developing a physical distribution system that is efficient and customer-oriented is a costly but vital process that can open new marketing opportunities.

Physical distribution is a prime consideration in analyzing market opportunities and identifying and designing market channels. In fact, since logistical consideration may represent major opportunities or constraints, physical distribution and market channel decisions are often made simultaneously.

Distribution decisions are a part of all phases of the strategic planning process, and distribution should be systematically planned and evaluated as a controllable variable. Decisions involve identifying both market opportunities and channel alternatives, since channel alternatives can determine which markets should be served and which marketing channels will be most efficient.

Physical distribution, which is a channel flow, is an integral part of providing the service and response levels, at acceptable or added value cost, target markets demand.

The elements of physical distribution include:

- Inventory.
- Transportation.
- Warehousing and materials handling.
- Communications and data processing.

How do you evaluate your system? Any evaluation requires clearly defined objectives. Objectives for distribution must support both organizational goals and marketing objectives. If your current physical distribution system can not meet the needs of your marketing strategy, options must be developed.

To compete effectively, your company must continue to lower costs while improving your ability to meet and even exceed customer demands. Although the initial investment is hefty, automated distribution centers employ bar coding technology, enable low-cost processing of large volumes, speed product to market, and provide accurate recording of inventory for tracking systems. A constant flow of communications throughout the organization as well as to customers or clients is essential to a supply chain model that is working at full capability.

Inbound logistics has a major impact on information system efficiencies. It can also be a major source of cost savings. Dollars saved on inbound costs go directly to your bottom line. Do you have a traffic department or at least one person functioning as a traffic cop? Set shipping requirements consistent with your strategic needs, then charge your traffic cop with finding the best rates possible within the framework of those requirements. Attention to outbound logistics, those activities involved in the transfer of goods/services to the customer once the decision to purchase has been made, can help save both you and your customers money.

The target customer's or client's perception of value and convenience is affected by how payment is taken and how goods and services are transferred. What message is your distribution operation sending? Is your distribution department able to provide your customers or your customer service people with real time information on the status of orders and inventory? Are you on your way to running a "paperless" warehouse operation? Is your warehouse management system capable of routinely providing same day shipping? Is it capable of handling increasing volumes of inventory without additional personnel? Do your distribution capabilities fit your strategic marketing plans and are they an integral part of your sales arsenal? If not, it's time to re-engineer your logistics and distribution to point your company toward the 21st century.

■ The Logistics of Service: Demand, Demand, Demand

We tend to think of logistics and distribution in relation to product manufacturers. The success of service businesses, however, depends upon delivering quickly. Speed, reliability, and often exclusivity are key elements in the distribution of services. In addition, services generally entail promotional and educational materials or supporting products that must be inventoried, warehoused, and trafficked. Speed and accuracy of information on order status is as vital for a service provider as for a product manufacturer.

Since many services are information- or entertainment-based, any technology that speeds that service on to the customer, such as on-line computing, 800 numbers, and pay-per-view television, must be considered as possible channels for physical distribution of your service—if they fit your vision, mission, and objectives!

JUMP START . . . .

1. Discuss how new and prospective channels of distribution will affect your physical distribution.
2. Discuss what changes you must make to your current systems in order to meet the changing demands of the marketplace.
3. Discuss how much it will cost to change. How much will it cost if you don't?

16

Training

The Continuous Tool

If you think education is expensive, try ignorance.

Derek Bok, author and former president
of Harvard University

Knowledge is power—the power that can keep your people up-to-date on the latest and greatest in technology, management techniques, thought leadership, and product knowledge. Even attending key conferences in order to network and share information is critical in these rapidly changing times.

Continuously improving the performance of your team is a very effective strategy for building and growing your company. Training is most effective when it is developed in response to a needs assessment that pinpoints the needs of each department and the various strata of personnel. Training should provide:

- Product and service knowledge.
- Techniques to help employees do their jobs better.

In addition training should ensure both better educated employees and better educated customers. Training for employees can be provided in various ways:

- Through vendors from whom you are buying a product, such as new software or new equipment.
- Through seminars given by training companies on specific technology and thought leadership.
- Through programs created in cooperation with community colleges.
- Through your own in-house educational programs.

Remember, without fuel a rocket ship can't move. It stays on the ground, rusts, and becomes outdated. Your people are your fuel; keep them charged to propel faster.

Training aimed at educating your customer/clients about your service or product should:

- Promote good will and create strategic alliances.
- Promote soft selling and thereby generate orders.
- Provide technical assistance.

Promoting strategic alliances is part of the strategic links process. Training your customer helps activate this process by enlisting rather than "selling" them. For training to provide strategic benefits, you must target the customers you want to train and appoint someone within your organization to spearhead the teaching modules and position the educational tools. What you choose to teach and how that training is presented reflects upon the image of your company. Before you proceed ask yourself, "Are our training programs in line with our vision, mission, and objectives?"

JUMP START . . . .

1. Do a needs assessment. Ask each team member what type of training their people need to better meet their department's goals and the mission and objectives of the company.
2. Explore alternative means of delivering training (videos, CD-ROMs, on-line, and teleconferencing).
3. Talk with vendors about what training they offer that relates to your needs.

17

The Top Line

I believe the power to make money is a gift of God.

John D. Rockefeller, as quoted in
Matthew Josephson's *The Robber Barons*

Throughout Part II you have been building your rocket ship link by strategic link. Once it is completed, you will need fuel to propel your rocket ship into the future. Your people are the fuel. They alone can grow your company's sales and profits and push gross margins and revenue enhancements to the *top.*

Profits are traditionally expressed as the bottom line. But profits don't trickle down, they are pushed to the top by the efforts of your team and all of your staff. So let's think out of the box, and begin to express profits in *top line* terms. Before we get to your top line—the ultimate measure of your success—let's look at a few significant measurements that will give you and your team a fresh way to appraise your company's efforts.

Volume Analysis

In Chapters 12 and 13, "Does the Product or Service Still Fit?" and "Channel Power: The Big Sell," we discussed a number of ways to analyze your sales volume—sales of products or services by territory, by individual product or service, by type of account, or by channel of distribution. While that's important information, it has one big limitation. It tells us nothing about profitability.

Profitability is indeed the top line. Profit growth rather than sales growth is the first objective in a marketing-oriented company. But there's more to know about profitability than your after-tax earnings figure. You need to know specifically how those profits are being generated. Which products and services, which territories, and which channels of distribution are contributing to the top line and to what degree? Without this knowledge, you have little control over your profit picture from quarter to quarter or year to year.

So wake up your curiosity and begin with a *marketing cost analysis.* A detailed study of the operating expense section of a company's profit & loss (P&L) statement, a marketing cost analysis can determine the relative profitability of territories, product/service lines, or other marketing units. For example, you may want to determine the profitability of a product sold through your own sales representatives compared with that of the same product sold through a sales rep firm. Understanding relative profitability can lead to important decisions regarding your team's choice of market channels. Or if you sell directly to consumers, you may want to calculate whether kiosk sales are more profitable than telemarketing sales. Such information is essential to planning your company's selling efforts.

Begin by establishing budgetary goals. Then compare your budgeted costs with actual expenses. Three different marketing cost analysis methodologies can help you reach a better understanding of your marketing function.

Analysis of Ledger Expenses

Using this methodology you can analyze "object of expenditure" costs as they appear in your P&L statement. Simply analyze each cost item (salaries, travel, and entertainment, etc.) in detail. Compare figures for the past three years to the current year, then make future projections. Bring members of your team together to discuss the trends over the years. Then ask: Can these costs be reallocated differently?

Again, compare your budgeted costs to your actual results. Then compute each expense as a percentage of net sales. Are you spending too much in one category, too little in another? How do you judge this? Compare your expense ratios with industry figures, which are frequently available from trade organizations, trade publications, annual reports, or your accounting firm.

Do you think your product or service deserves greater market penetration? Perhaps you are not investing adequately in some aspect of marketing. You can get a good indication by comparing your expense ratios with those of other companies or with industry averages. Do you find, for example that your company is spending 1 percent of sales on advertising and promotion, while your industry's average is 3 percent? If so, you may need to reexamine your expenditures in this category.

Analysis of Functional Expenses

The point of any expense analysis is to gather more information than is available from a ledger account analysis alone. A ledger account analysis will not establish the cost effectiveness of databasing and other New Marketing tools, because the information provided is too broad. But with functional expense analyses, you can look more closely at your company's expenses. An analysis of activity expenses in total also provides an excellent starting point for more focused analyses such as costs by territories, products or services, or other marketing units. An analysis of functional expenses may also prompt you to look at costs differently to see where added value is important. Are customer service or loyalty programs providing the added value you expect? Are consumer focus groups or chat lines established through the Internet providing added value? Are the expenses justified by the top line?

Certainly your company's new strategic directions and LINKS demand that costing allocations be thought out differently. With each department or division linked to the next, expenses that were once allocated to a single department or division will now be shared. You will only have a true picture of each department or division's profitability if these expenses are allocated accurately.

How do you start? Select appropriate groups of activities, then allocate each ledger expense among those activities. Allocating costs requires careful thought. Some items, such as the costs of media space, can be apportioned directly to one activity—advertising. Other expenses must be prorated, but only after the team has established some reasonable basis for allocation. Property taxes, for instance, may be allocated according to the proportion of total floor space occupied by each department or division. Allocation of general office salaries and expenses could require an analysis of each department or division's use of general office services. Such an analysis should be updated as each department's needs change and grow. In some companies, expenses for electricity could be fairly based on each department's total floor space. In others, where there is heavier use of computers or machinery in certain departments or divisions, proper allocation requires more study.

Analysis of Functional Costs by Market Segments

The third and most beneficial type of marketing cost analysis is a study of the costs and profitability of each segment of the market. Commonly the market is examined by territories, products/services, customer groups, or order sizes. Using a cost analysis by market segment, the team is able to pinpoint troubled areas much more effectively than if they were simply analyzing ledger-account expenses or activity costs. For example, ledger account expenses will not reveal whether a consumer foods producer's sales of salsa to inner city bodegas is as profitable as sales to large regional supermarkets. Nor will analyzing activity costs show whether sales of maintenance contracts on appliances are more profitable in the Northeast than in the Midwest. But analyzing functional costs by market areas brings "trouble spots" into focus allowing you to reallocate, rethink, and change them.

By combining sales volume analysis with a marketing cost study, a company can prepare a complete operating statement for each of its product/service or market segments. Analyzing these individual statements can determine the effectiveness of the marketing program as it relates to each segment and allows the company to respond faster to market needs.

The procedure for making a cost analysis by market segments is similar to that used to analyze functional or activity expenses. The total of each activity cost (which can be rethought) is prorated to each product or market segment being studied. For example, it can be prorated to such activity cost groups as advertising, warehousing and shipping, order processing and billing, marketing administration, or one-on-one selling.

■ Aim for Accurate Allocations

A marketing cost analysis requires time, money, and manpower. The task of allocating costs is particularly difficult and requires a thinking-out-of-the-box mentality. You are aiming to develop a true picture of profitability for all segments of your company and your business. Since your company and your markets are continually changing, you must regularly review and update your allocations. If you are gathering information and responding in real time, your allocations will be more accurate and your opportunities to maximize profits will be greater.

Taking a Strategic Links approach to your business complicates the allocation process. Research and development (R&D), for example, can no longer be treated as an insular division with well defined expenses. Today technology is an enabler for all areas of the company from manufacturing, marketing, sales, warehousing and shipping to changing channels of distribution. For example, if your R&D staff develops an information and communications system that all company divisions can tie into, then that expense should be borne by each division. To properly allocate your R&D expenses, your team must consider each of these newly forged links.

The complexity of allocating costs becomes most evident when you begin to apportion activity costs among individual territories, products, services, or other marketing units. Operating costs can be divided into direct and indirect expenses. Salary and travel expenses incurred in conjunction with one market segment are direct expenses and are therefore easily allocated.

Indirect or common costs cannot be charged totally to one market segment and therefore present a challenge. To complicate the process further, some costs are *partially* indirect and some are *totally* indirect. For example, order filling and shipping are partial, while marketing and administrative expenses are totally indirect. With order filling and shipping, that portion of their activities related directly to a department or division can be allocated directly, the remainder of the expense must be allocated based on the judgment of the team working with the account department. The allocation of marketing and administration expenses are totally based on the team's judgment. Making these allocation decisions isn't easy, but they are essential to understanding your profitability.

■ Full Costs versus Contribution-Margin

Two popular methods for allocating expenses are demonstrated in Exhibit 17–1. In the *contribution-margin* approach, only direct expenses are allocated to each marketing unit being analyzed. These are costs that presumably would be eliminated if that marketing unit were eliminated. When these direct expenses are deducted from the gross margin of the marketing unit, the remainder is that unit's contribution to total indirect expenses or overhead.

For example, assume you operate an accounting firm that services small businesses, but also prepares income taxes for the general public. To allocate expenses for the income tax division, using the contribution-margin approach, you would include salaries for the division as well as any mailing, faxing, stationery, phone, or other expenses directly attributed

FULL COST	CONTRIBUTION-MARGIN
Sales $$	Sales $$
– Cost of Goods Sold	– Cost of Goods Sold
= Gross Margin	= Gross Margin
– Direct and	– Direct Expenses
Indirect Expenses	
= THE NET PROFIT	= CONTRIBUTION-MARGIN
	(the amount available to cover overhead expenses plus a profit)

Exhibit 17–1
Full Cost vs. Contribution Margin

to the division. Should you close the income tax division, those expenses, and only those expenses, would be eliminated. You would not allocate such expenses as a percentage of administrative or general office salaries that remain even if the division closes.

In the *full-cost* approach, all expenses, direct and indirect, are allocated among the marketing units being studied. By allocating all costs, management or the team can determine the net profit of each territory, product/service, or other marketing unit. The full-cost approach, for example, allows a company to focus more precisely on the profitability of a growing product or service as new territories or markets are added. A cleaning product, for example, that is sold through independent hardware stores will demonstrate a different profitability profile if it is sold through mass merchandisers. The full-cost approach will allow you to consider such variables as mark-up, warehousing, shipping, advertising, and promotion when assessing profitability.

■ Now What? Making Decisions Based on Combined Volume and Cost Analyses

Marketing cost analysis is only the first stage of the evaluation process. During that phase, you learn about what has happened. Now you are ready to look at examples of how the team could use results from a combined sales volume analysis and marketing cost analysis to make decisions about the company's future.

Territorial/Service Decisions

Changing channels of distribution are forcing companies to reconsider territories and levels of service. Only when management or the team knows the net profit or contribution to overhead of the territories in relations to their potential, can they take action. Action plans may include:

1. *Adjusting (expanding or contracting) territories* to bring them into line with current sales potential. A company may decide that certain states offer too little sales potential to justify the number of sales representatives currently servicing the area. As a result of the cost analysis, the company may assign the territory to a single sales representative, then back the rep with a telemarketing effort. The object is to realize a greater profit margin while maintaining or possibly increasing sales.

2. *Making changes in distribution* if territorial issues stem from weaknesses in "channel power." If you are selling a service to business customers at trade shows and conventions, waning attendance and a need to be in contact with your customers on a more regular basis may prompt a decision to sell directly to your customers over the Internet. The new technology may prove to be far more cost efficient than exhibiting at trade shows with the attendant travel, hotel, and entertainment expenses. In addition, the new marketing channel could provide new customers and increased purchasing frequency among current customers. The combination of increased sales and trimmed costs will have a positive effect on your company's top line.

3. *Changing the marketing and promotion program* if intensive competition appears to be the cause of unprofitable volume. Companies can only counter intensive competition by reaching a better understanding of consumer/customer needs. New strategies and marketing tools such as databasing and research, which provide a better understanding of consumer/customer needs, can give a company the competitive edge that turns unprofitable volume into top-line profits. Therefore, marketing and promotion programs should be highly responsive to changing customer needs.

4. *Abandoning a losing territory* completely. If consumer/customer research demonstrates that a territory is losing share of market or has little hope of profitability, abandoning the territory may be the only answer. Again,

profitability is your top line. Sometimes territories—as well as products, services, and channels of distribution—must be discontinued in order to move into the future. None of these profit-building territory/service decisions can be reached unless you have developed marketing costs analyses and other measures of profitability.

Product/Service Decision

When you know the relative profitability of each product, service, or group of products or services, you may choose to simplify the product/service line by eliminating slow moving or unprofitable models or services. You may elect to restructure sales compensation to encourage sales of the core competencies or high margin products. Channels of distribution may be altered. For example, instead of selling all products to retailers, you might elect to sell directly to consumers on the Internet. Before making these decisions, however, the team must consider the effect of each action. For example, would a decision to sell on the Internet require a change in pricing structure? And how would the company's business processes need to change to accommodate doing business in real time, which speeds your product or service to market.

■ EVA/MVA: A New Way of Looking at Your Top Line

Finally let's look at your company's *Economic Value Added* (EVA) and *Market Value Added* (MVA)—new concepts, developed by Stern Stewart, the New York City-based financial consulting firm. MVA, simply stated, measures whether management has increased or decreased the value of the capital invested by shareholders and lenders.

Stern Stewart's MVA model adds up all the capital a company has received from equity and debt offerings, bank loans, and retained earnings then adjusts for capitalization of research and development and spending as an investment in future earnings. The final result is compared with the current value of the company stock and debt.

Total market value less Invested capital = Market value added

In other words, MVA is the dollar value of the wealth that has been created by the company's management. A minus figure demonstrates capital that has been wasted or misspent. EVA focuses on the after tax operating profit less the company's cost of capital for that year. EVA offers an entirely new way of evaluating the top line by showing how much wealth a company has created within a given year.

Coca-Cola, a Stern Stewart client, is considered the world's top wealth producer with $60.8 billion in Market Value Added. Microsoft is coming up fast. Ten years ago the software company didn't even make the MVA list. In 1996, it was number five on the MVA list.

Companies can create negative MVA and EVA too. Let's consider a simple analysis of two hypothetical companies—both in the consumer foods business. Firm number one, the Holy Moley Sauce Company, launches a line of Mexican-inspired sauces. The second company, Cold Comfort Frozen Desserts, debuts a fat-free, sugar-free, lactose-free imitation ice cream. Both invest $50 million in bank loans and stock offerings. After three years of strong growth, the Holy Moley Sauce Company realizes net profits of $8 million on a sales volume of $65 million. Most important, the value of the company's stock—its total market value is $120 million. Subtract the $50 million initial investment for $70 million MVA.

Cold Comfort, on the other hand has built a $65 million volume with profits of $6 million. A cursory look at the two company's ledgers would suggest that they've both grown at the same pace. But Cold Comfort's stock is valued at only

$40 million. Subtract the $50 million investment from stock-holders and bank loans and Cold Comfort has a minus MVA of $10 million. Bad management decisions at Cold Comfort have wasted capital, while sound decisions at Holy Moley have created wealth.

■ The Top Line vs. The Bottom Line

Planning may be defined as drawing information from the *past*, then redefining or moving the pieces of information and the Strategic Links into different positions in order to decide in the *present* what to do for the *future*. The findings from analyses such as these are extremely helpful in shaping decisions to think out of the box and creating new links to market into the future—while keeping your top line in focus.

JUMP START . . . .

1. Explain how the results of a territorial sales volume analysis may influence a firm's promotional program. What effects may a sales volume analysis by product or service have on training, supervising, and compensating the salesforce?

2. Firms should discontinue selling losing products or services. Do you agree with that statement? Discuss with your team the circumstances under which products or services should be discontinued.

3. Should a company discontinue selling to an unprofitable customer? Why? Why not? If not, what steps might the company take to make the account a profitable one?

18

Measurements for Success

Is the Team Meeting Its Goals?

One must learn by doing the thing; though you think you know it, you have no certainty until you try.

Sophocles, *Trachiniae*

Okay! So you and your strategic assessment team have almost completed the Strategic Value Chain, tying each of the links back to your vision, mission and key objectives. You're just about ready to make it all happen. But you ask yourself: How will we know if it *is* happening? How can we monitor our progress? How can we know whether we should make adjustments?

After you set your strategic objectives, you must formulate tactical goals, which will be discussed in depth in Part III. These shorter term goals measure team performances related to specific tasks. Each goal is aimed at bringing you closer to your vision, mission and overall objectives. In monitoring performance, put technology to work for you. Software programs are available to help with this process. Or you can set up your own system which should include a time line, expected goals, and a record of the people or teams that are responsible for them. Ask those people to report their progress link by link, week to week, or month by month.

Use a time line or Gantt chart (Exhibit 18–1) to help keep projects moving on time and to let your teams understand how their tasks fit into the overall project. Also put these controls on computer so that your team can refer to them at any time.

If no monitoring system is in place, neither team leaders nor corporate management will be able to assess how things are going or where the problem areas are. Goal monitoring and other measurements for success provide management with increased capability to react to business and environmental changes in a timely manner. It will help management achieve its corporate mission—whether that mission is growth or downsizing—by providing the on-going feedback

	JAN	FEB	MAR	APR	MAY	JUNE	JULY	AUG
Vision								
Mission								
Culture Factor								
Framework for the Future								
Organization								
Operations								
The New Consumerism								
New Marketing								

Exhibit 18–1
Time Table—Gantt Chart

necessary for employees to adjust their actions so that all activities contribute to common goals. Goal monitoring also creates a collaborative environment and enables objective, real time performance appraisals on an on-going basis. Your people want and need performance feedback to gain insight into where they are in the process.

JUMP START . . . .

1. Discuss and agree on goals for each department. All goals must support the mission and the objectives.
2. Set objective standards that measure both quality of performance and ability to meet deadlines.
3. Monitor performance and provide feedback and coaching to keep people on track.

19

Make It Happen!

Measurements for Control

Problems are only opportunities in work clothes.

Henry J. Kaiser, American industrialist

Once your ideas are in place and you start to move through the different processes of your business, then controls must be put in place. The objective of the controls is to create a checks and balances system that will catch various situations, problems, issues, or business transactions that may interfere with changes being instituted properly.

Let's take you away from your business to better understand what we mean by the control process. You are at home and have discovered you are out of milk. You need to go to the store to buy a quart. Simple task, but what could go wrong along the way?

1. You have no money.
2. You can't find your car keys.
3. There's no gas in the car.
4. You get a flat tire on the way.

5. You get a speeding ticket.
6. The road is washed out and you have to detour.
7. You have an accident en route.
8. You get to the store and discover your wallet is at home.
9. The store is closed.
10. The store is open, but out of milk.

When a task is as simple as buying one quart of milk, chances are you will be successful. But life is seldom that simple and your business *never* is. So buy yourself some insurance and institute controls. Consider how controls would have helped in the pursuit of a quart of milk.

Before	*Control Action*
1. No money.	Be aware of your money situation at all times. Keep some cash on hand at home.
2. Can't find your car keys.	Keep your car keys in the same place or keep a second set of keys.
3. No gas in the car.	Check your gas level at regular intervals. Always buy gas when the tank is half empty.
4. You get a flat tire.	Keep a spare in the trunk. Inspect tires regularly.
5. You get a speeding ticket.	Never drive over the speed limit.
6. The road is washed out.	Be aware of all weather and travel conditions.
7. You have an accident.	Slow down! Take a driving training course.
8. Your wallet is at home.	Never leave home without it.

Before	*Control Action*
9. The store is closed.	Phone ahead.
10. The store is out of milk.	While you're calling ask if they have milk.

Many of life's little fiascos could be avoided if we just paid attention to detail. Creating measurements for control is similar to going through the LINKS process. You are asking yourself: What if? What could go wrong? And what can we do so that it doesn't go wrong? Providing controls aimed at creating a better, more reliable flow of transactions and processes ensures that your strategic plan will happen and that you will meet your vision, mission, and objectives. Then you can spend your time strategizing rather than putting out fires.

JUMP START . . . .

---

1. For each project or activity, discuss the possible problems and pitfalls that might arise.
2. Find preventive actions that can help your people avoid most problems.
3. Encourage similar planning at every level of your business.

PART III

THINKING OUT OF THE BOX

Let's Get Specific

We've discussed strategy and strategic planning throughout the last 19 chapters. Now it's time to think about *tactics,* the real "how to" specifics that can put your plan into action. *Tactics* is defined as "the technique or science of securing the objectives designated by strategy," according to *The American Heritage Dictionary,* while a *tactic* is "an expedient for achieving a goal; a maneuver."

The next three chapters are exactly that—expedients or maneuvers for implementing a Strategic Marketing Plan that actuates your corporate vision and creates added value. Along the way you will learn to use the tools that will help you navigate through each of the Strategic Links.

Imagine that your Strategic Links look like The LINKS (Leverage Ideas to Navigate Key Strategies) Game (Exhibit III–1). While the LINKS in the game follow one another, just as chapters 4 through 19 follow one another, there really is no single route or "correct" way to navigate your company into the Future. Rather than go from Link 6 to 7 to 8 to 9, you may jump from 1 to 7 and then return to link 3 or 6. For example, you could move directly from the Mission Link into Real Time, then return to the Culture Factor.

No one can give you a road map, because you and your team must trailblaze your own path. Like the information superhighway, your road to the future is nonlinear. You will

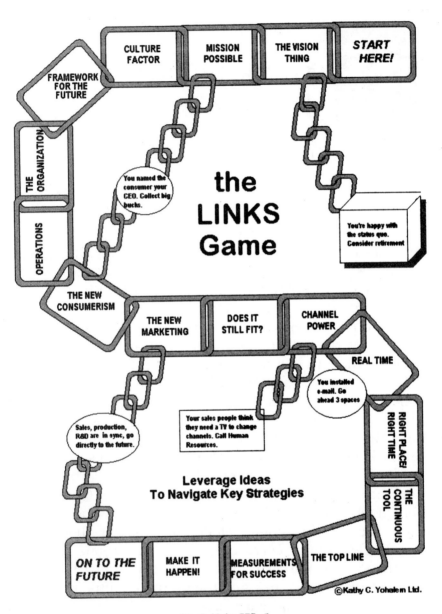

Exhibit III–1
The LINKS Game

also explore side roads on the road to the future. Consider them day trips or excursions that will give you additional tools to move ahead. Nothing that you learn or explore is wasted. It is experience and knowledge you can store for future use.

So begin moving into the future one link at a time, adding whichever link works best for you next. To reach your future, you must explore each link in the Strategical Value Chain. Watch out for pitfalls, but move ahead fearlessly link by link until you have built your chain into the future. You've already made your start. Now begin to move ahead by trying out the tactics in Chapters 20 to 22 that will make all the theory come alive for you.

20

FOCUS

KISS

A journey of a thousand miles begins with a single step.

Chinese Proverb

Just put one foot in front of the other. It's simple, stupid. If you've never practiced KISS tactics (Keep It Simple, Stupid), this is the time to start. We may get a bit lofty plotting our strategies, but tactics and implementation require simplicity. This chapter and the following two chapters offer tactical, hands-on solutions to achieving your company's goals. These tactics are logical, essential, and simple. Keep them that way.

The implementation of a strategic marketing plan, like all journeys, begins with a single step. The problem is, with so much to do, what is that first step? Reshaping a company is an enormous undertaking. Even when top management has a good idea where it is going, getting there can be extremely complex.

So where do you begin? With planning—both long- and short-term. Actualizing a new marketing

149

strategy usually takes at least a year. A company could spend four months or longer concentrating on strategy—depending on the size and complexity of the company and how much reorganization is involved. During this time, the company begins by focusing on the LINKS process (see "How to Find Your Competitive Advantage," Chapter 3). The strategic assessment team first discovers the company's opportunities, then moves on to its vision, mission, and objectives.

The implementation portion requires at least eight months, again depending on the size of the company. Implementation is done in pieces, link by link, with each link subject to its own time frame. Some links may require continuous, ongoing work; others might be satisfactorily completed in weeks. Be aware that as you make changes in one area, department, or division of the company, other areas will also be affected—some more acutely than others.

■ Take Action: The Planning Calendar

Get this process rolling by committing your action plan to paper. Start a planning calendar such as the one in Exhibit 20–1. Using this planning calendar, you and your strategic assessment team will guide your company through each link in the strategic assessment process. Your team will work through each of the 16 Strategic Links discussed in Chapters 4 through 19 from "The Vision Thing" through "Make it Happen! Measurements for Control." Moving through each of the links will quickly demonstrate how one change can affect nearly every segment of your company.

Let's look at how it works. Begin with the task at hand. Column 1, in the ten-column planning calendar, describes the link you and your team will attack—vision, mission, etc. Here you indicate the link you are working on. Next, decide which team members will work on that particular link. For links, such as the vision or "The Culture Factor," you will probably want to involve all team members. Other links may be assigned to only a few members. In column 2 list the names of the team members who will be involved in each link. Column 3 simply describes the area of the company each member represents.

Various tasks must be addressed as you and your team explore each link. For example, in working through the mission link, several team members may be assigned to do research, while others may be involved the actual writing of the statement. Use column 4 to describe the assignments that each team member will undertake.

An important part of planning is setting time limits. Columns 5 though 8 of the planning calendar are used to record important dates—start date, due date (the day the committee is expected to present their initial findings), review/approval date, and decision date (the day the team will either approve or table actions).

After you have made decisions concerning an individual link—whether it is the "New Marketing," the "Organization," or "Real Time," you will be able to make assumptions about what must happen next and how your decisions will affect other segments of the company. Column 9 in the planning calendar is reserved for assumptions. If the team decides to follow action A, what assumptions follow? What must be done next? How will the decision affect various areas of the company? Finally, you will create an action plan. What will the team do to enact their decisions? Briefly describe the action plan in column 10. The planning calendar keeps everyone in focus and on track. Maintain it throughout the tactical process, and remember to keep it simple.

■ Working Through the LINKS Game—Link by Strategic Link

Your next task is to thoroughly understand all of the ramifications of your actions. Begin by making a list of the objectives you want to accomplish. As you look over your list of objectives, you and your team should ask: What? Why? Where? When? Who? How?

Objective	Team Member	Department	Assignment	Start Date	Due Date
Step 1-LINKs Process	J. McCarthy	Marketing	group works LINKS process	1/10/97	2/15/97
	A. Phillips	Sales	"		
	K. Myruski	Production	"		
	L. Abrams	R & D	"		
	T. Rodriguez	Distribution	"		
	M. Scott	Pres. CEO	"		
Step 2-VISION	A. Phillips	Sales	customer, field research		
	K. Myruski	Production	internal research		
	L. Abrams	R & D	research, technology impact		
	T. Rodriguez	Distribution	point person, organize, etc.		
	M. Scott	Pres. CEO	write statement		
	J. McCarthy	Marketing	write statement		
Step 3-Mission					

Exhibit 20-1
Planning Calendar

Review/Approval Date	Decision Date	Assumptions	Action Plan
3/15/97	3/30/97		

For example, assume that one of your objectives is to provide laptop computers to your sales representatives. The laptops are your *what*. *Who* other than the sales reps will receive laptops? Support personnel? Sales managers? Major customers? And *who* will be tied into the information system? Then ask *why* you are taking this action. Is it so your sales reps can go on-line to provide customers with accurate inventory information? So they can make marketing presentations on CD-ROMs? So they can give customers information and process orders in real time? Do you expect sales reps to communicate with other company personnel via e-mail?

Where will the laptops be used? In the field? At home? In the office? *When* do you plan to inaugurate the laptop system? *How* will you meet that time frame? And *how* will you approach the project? *How* will the software be created? And *how much* will it all cost? *What* will it do to your top line and how much added value will it provide?

Now take your understanding of the ramifications of the laptops even further by moving through each of the 16 Strategic Links that you visited in Chapters 4 through 19. By doing this, you can see how the laptops will affect every area of your company. Decisions, such as the implementation of laptop technology, should never be made without understanding how that change will affect each link in the company and how it will affect top line results

To see how this can work, let's put it into action. Using the laptops, we'll work through each of the 16 Strategic Links. As you and your team move through the links you will see how the acquisition of the laptops by your sales department will affect everything from the vision and mission to your "Top Line" (see Exhibit 20–2). Now, keeping it simple, go link by link from the present to the future.

- *The vision thing.* Your vision statement is your expression of what you and your strategic marketing

Exhibit 20–2
Laptops: A Link to Your Future

team agree your company could and can be. Laptops will provide real time customer information that will enable your current vision and expand future visions. Consider your company's vision statement. How would laptops enable it? How do you think you could reshape your vision after introducing laptops?

- *Mission possible.* A mission statement defines the company's arena of business, its customers, and its objectives for the future. The laptops help define your customers more accurately by speeding information on their needs, thereby enabling your company to reach its objectives more rapidly.

- *The culture factor.* A negative corporate culture is often the result of too little communications—particularly from the bottom up. The laptops are a new way of doing business that disseminates information quickly and more openly. The laptops will let light and air into a stuffy, staid corporate culture. As with any change in your corporate culture, expect resistance and be prepared to deal with it.

- *Infrastructure: Framework for the future.* The laptops change the way you work with your in-house people and your customers. The information laptops provide can assist in determining whether your infrastructure and its SBUs are properly structured.

- *Organization.* In a well-structured organization, information flows back and forth from department to department and from top to bottom. The laptops will tie your organization together through new information links.

- *Operations: A strategic tool.* Operations consists of all the activities involved in the selling of the product or service up to the taking of payment from the client. The laptops are a strategic tool that enhances and speeds that process. They help assure that your operations presents a homogeneous image, that product arrival will be more consistent, and that everyone in operations is on the same wave length.

- *The New Consumerism.* Suddenly you are talking to your customers in a different way, allowing them to interface directly with your company. You are moving closer to Consumer Demand Response—a totally integrated supply chain with multiple information flows— that will allow you to speed the right product or service to market. Your laptops will also provide some of the consumer/customer information you need for databasing and datamining which will help predict future demand. With laptops your company is listening and responding.

- *The New Marketing.* Information, information, information. That's what the New Marketing is all about. You now have more information faster than ever before. The laptops will also help you achieve the *integrated marketing* that assures everyone in the company is working toward the same goals, image, and knowledge rather than working in independent directions.

- *Does the product or service still fit?* If you didn't know before, you can't miss it now. By doing business in real time, the laptops will speed up your assessment of current products and services and provide the consumer/customer input needed to consider new products and services.

- *Channel power: The big sell.* In addition to helping you service your current customers better, laptops are an important tool in opening up new channels of distribution. For example, they are an essential piece in opening up mass merchandising opportunities. In addition, they facilitate the four-step sales process: prospecting, qualifying, developing, and closing. They also help the representatives plan strategies for their regions, execute their plans, and control the progress of those plans.

- *Real time.* Your information systems department will integrate the laptops into your existing information systems. They should make certain the laptop software links with accounting, your warehouse management system, and other areas of the company.

- *Getting it to the right place at the right time.* New warehouse management systems are speeding product and services to market, while interchanging information with customer service and other areas of the company. The acquisition of the laptops will further speed those products and services by providing one more link in the information chain.

- *Training the continuous tool.* Alert human resources. They will have to provide training to everyone using the laptop technology, including the executives and support personnel who work with the sales reps, your customer service department, and order fulfillment. Never forget that it's your people who make change work.

- *The top line.* That's the whole point. If an action doesn't ultimately have a positive effect on your profits, forget it. While the laptops represent an investment in hardware, software, and training, they should provide substantial savings while spurring sales.

- *Measurements for success—Is the team meeting its goals?* Your laptops will enable you to measure how well your team is meeting its tactical goals. They will help by providing the on-going feedback that is necessary for your staff to adjust their actions so their activities contribute to meeting the company's vision and mission statement.

- *Make it happen! Measurements for control.* As we said before, many of life's little fiascos could be avoided if we paid attention to detail. The laptops enable you to see the details, put them into a cohesive framework, and track the business processes and goals.

■ FOCUS: First Things First

Only after you and your team have taken each objective through the What, Where, Why, When, Who, and How process and have worked through each of the links are you ready to begin prioritizing your objectives. Using the FOCUS quadrant shown in Exhibit 20–3, ask, "Which of these objectives are 1st priority and which are 2nd priority?" Then ask, "Which can be accomplished internally and which will require external cooperation or strategic alliances?"

Begin assigning each of your objectives to the proper quadrant. Some objectives are more important than others. Some must be realized first to facilitate others. Internal

FOCUS		
	1st Priority	**2nd Priority**
Internal	Quadrant I	Quadrant II
External	Quadrant III	Quadrant IV

Exhibit 20–3
Focus

objectives, such as a companywide e-mail system can usually be realized more quickly than those that require external cooperation, such as a just-in-time system which requires cooperation from both suppliers and customers.

When you have finished, make a list of the objectives in each of the four quadrants and further prioritize each list. Your objective is to be sure each piece or link is easily and logically implemented. Assume, for example, that you want to introduce e-mail, laptops, and Internet customer service. Take each of these objectives through a series of "what if" scenarios with the aim of prioritizing your activities so that each objective or link fits.

As you and your team begin employing these tactics, keep in mind the precepts we discussed earlier. Think out of the box and keep your curiosity level high.

As a team you should also remember:

- *Think long term.* You are creating your company's future, rather than looking for a quick fix.
- *Think as a team with a collective view.* You are reshaping your entire company, rather than patching up a department or division.
- *People, people, people.* They are your most important asset. Train them, nurture them, and give them opportunities for growth within your framework for change.
- *Start with drivers of change.* Ask, for example: How does the Internet/Web affect your industry? What do your customers need that might not be in the market yet?
- *Create new patterns; challenge old patterns.* That means asking questions such as how could we do it differently? You will be looking to create new paradigms that change all the old assumptions. Frequently as we think out of the box to find new paradigms, we find technology is the enabler. As with the laptops, that technology may change every aspect of your company.

Finally ask yourself:

- How are we challenging old systems of information?
- What are the alternatives? (To everything.)
- Are we open? (To everything.)
- Are we using KISS tactics?

21

Strategic Design

A Map for Success

The crucial question is: "What comes first?" rather than "What should be done?" . . . The normal human reaction is to evade the priority decision by doing a little bit of everything.

Peter Drucker, management consultant,
writer, and professor

In Chapter 20, you and your team organized your planning calendar and took your list of objectives through each of the Strategic Links to learn how changes affect every aspect of your business. Then you prioritized your objectives. Now, let's get tactical about designing your strategy. Using a model called "The Links in Strategy Design" (see Exhibit 21–1), you will design the step-by-step strategy that will create added value and propel your company and its products/services into the future. You begin with a vision that is taken through a series of Strategic Links resulting in profitability. Let's take this one link at a time.

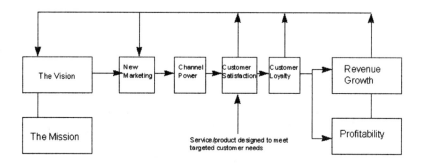

What Is Your Company's Added Value?

Exhibit 21–1
The Links in Strategy Design

■ Tactics for Strategy Design

1. *The vision and mission.* The starting point for any company is its vision and mission. Without direction your company will go nowhere. Whether you are plotting out objectives such as the acquisition of laptops, planning for new products or services, or looking to go global, everything flows from the vision and mission.

2. *The strategic assessment links.* In our model, the major Strategic Links are "The New Marketing" and "Channel Power." Here is where *added value* is created. (Of course, other links, such as "Real Time," "The New Consumerism," and "Getting It to the Right Place at the Right Time" also add value.) The process of adding value through the Strategic Links works much as any manufacturing process in which raw materials are refined and shaped into a finished product.

As an example, let's use the trade magazine publisher who worked through the LINKS process before acquiring a fax machine. Our publisher decided to buy faxes for each of his offices, which helped propel him from yesterday into the present. Now he is looking to move into the future with new technology and new products. His raw materials are ideas that must be processed and distributed in some form. His editors, writers, and art directors add value to those ideas by shaping them into articles, photographs, and illustrations. His printer (or CD-ROM producer) adds even greater value by placing the editorial materials into a format that can be distributed to the reading audience.

If he is wise, he uses the precepts of the New Marketing— observing the changing tastes and needs of his audience and his advertisers. He stays aware of changing technology that may affect the way he brings his products to market. Then he brands his products with logos which over time have come to represent a standard of quality and reliability in both his readers' and advertisers' minds.

Channel Power has just begun to open up for our publisher. Until recently, he felt his channels were limited to selling advertisers and reaching audiences via a printed format. Now the Internet, CD-ROM magazines, and ancillary products offer the publisher new ways to reach audiences and new products to sell.

3. *Customer satisfaction* is a major objective. First he must satisfy customer number 1—the reading audience. If that audience is assured, then customer number 2—the advertiser—will likely be satisfied as well.

4. *Customer loyalty* is created through long-term customer satisfaction and continuing improvement of the publisher's products. With customer loyalty, the publisher can create brand extension through new channels and ancillary products. He can also create new publications based on his company's reputation.

5. *Revenue growth* is one reward. The publisher's business thrives as he satisfies his customers and builds a loyal customer base. Sales grow through additional readers and advertisers and through new products and services.

6. *Profitability* is his final reward. If the publisher has added value throughout the process—keeping an eye on the top line, the finished products and services he offers his customers have far greater value than the raw material with which he started.

Creating strategy design that adds value in today's business world is not as complicated as it first appears. Apply your vision or mission to move a product or service through the Strategic Links adding value as you go. Use the precepts you learned in the New Marketing and Channel Power (as well as Real Time, the New Consumerism, and other links) to create added value in products and services that meet targeted customer needs. Satisfy your customers consistently to build customer loyalty. Apply the step-by-step tactics of the planning calendar, work each product through the 16 Strategic Links, and use the FOCUS quadrant to ease the process. The result: revenue growth and profitability.

■ Tactics for Strategic Assessment

The next step is to assess the company and its strategies from all aspects. (See Exhibit 21–2.) First you will do a complete Business Assessment from five perspectives , then you will move to the opposite side of our model and look at the Critical Success Factors and Business Requirements.

Begin attacking your Strategic Assessment by assigning various team members to each of the following:

1. *Current strategy* scrutinizes the formal and informal strategies your company is currently attempting. What are those strategies, and how are they articulated by each of your team members and each department of your company?

2. *Market analysis* examines the marketplace. What are your dataminers saying about your market? What is

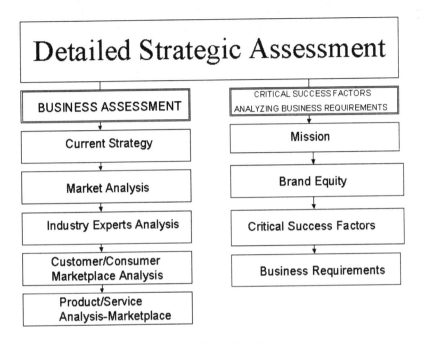

Detailed Strategic Assessment

BUSINESS ASSESSMENT	CRITICAL SUCCESS FACTORS ANALYZING BUSINESS REQUIREMENTS
Current Strategy	Mission
Market Analysis	Brand Equity
Industry Experts Analysis	Critical Success Factors
Customer/Consumer Marketplace Analysis	Business Requirements
Product/Service Analysis-Marketplace	

Exhibit 21–2
Detailed Strategic Assessment

its potential for growth and how is it changing. How will your products or services fit into this changing market in the years ahead?

3. *Industry experts analysis* will reflect the ideas and opinions of industry leaders. How do leading competitors in your industry articulate their view of the market? What do prime retailers, distributors, industry association leaders, and other industry affiliates think?

4. *Customer/Consumer marketplace analysis* examines what your best customers and potential customers think.

5. And finally during *Product/Service analysis* you will analyze the current status of your products and

services, gathering the opinions and ideas of your sales, marketing, and product/service development people.

Let's illustrate this procedure, again using the magazine publishing company. How would the company assess its current business? The publisher and his strategic assessment team would look at its employees; its monetary assets and liabilities; its marketing, sales, editorial, and technological capabilities.

To assess current strategy, they would examine where the company is trying to go and what its growth objectives are in terms of new publications and collateral businesses.

In market analysis they would look at the various markets its publications serve. As a publisher of trade magazines (publications serving specific industries), the company would assess new directions for the businesses each publication serves.

The publisher and his team would undertake two industry experts analyses. First they would turn to experts in the markets their publications serve to understand how their readers needs and tastes are changing and how the latest trends and technology are affecting that industry and the way their competitors are doing business. Next they would turn to industry experts in the communications field to learn where the business of publishing is going—technologically, legally, aesthetically. They would seek to learn about new business practices and new training procedures being adopted by others in the field.

The customer/consumer marketplace analysis would try to learn more about how the company's advertisers think. More importantly, the company would learn how its readers—the advertisers' customers—think so that the publisher can be seen as an authority on the market.

When the publisher and his team have finished with these analyses and assessments, the next step is a product/

service analysis. How well do the publisher's products and services fit the needs of the market, the readers, and the advertisers?

Once the assessment is completed, the company is ready to move to the right side of the Detailed Strategic Assessment model. Only then is the team able to determine the critical success factors needed to create a good business.

1. *Mission.* By understanding the analysis pieces and arriving at conclusions, the team can then formulate a mission statement, substantiate its current mission, or update it.

2. *Brand equity.* Having developed or refined the mission, the team is prepared to look at brand equity with a better understanding of market needs, customer needs, industry viewpoints and the company's current strategy. They finally have the information needed to act.

3. *Critical success factors.* The team can now ask: What are the critical success factors that our company needs to accomplish a good business?

4. *Business requirements.* Finally, what is required of the business to achieve the mission, create the critical success factors, and achieve the company's objectives?

Both the Links in Strategy Design and the Detailed Strategic Assessment charts are KISS tactics that works. Just take them one step at time moving link by link.

22

Take Control!

If anything can go wrong—it will.

One of Murphy's laws

You and your team must communicate and track every change you make. If you don't communicate— both internally and externally—your objectives will never be realized. Remember, neither your people nor your customers are mind readers. And, if you don't track what is happening, neither you nor your team will know whether your efforts are successful.

We accept many methods for tracking success including measurements such as ROI, net profits, and sales volume (to the extent that it's profitable). So too, a company must have measurements of control if it wants to monitor performance and profitability while easing the way for ROI. But what do you measure? How do you measure it . . . and keep track of it? And how frequently should you measure it?

Create goal tracking charts. Keep them on computer so each department can monitor its progress. Only then can you effectively challenge your infrastructure to reflect business practices needed for the 21st century. Keep records of the planning process, as well as competitive or business strategies, strategic interrelationships and alliances, and ways that you create added value. Create measurements for the costs of creating value through shared activities and through transferred skills.

The following questions will give you a jump start and get the thinking process moving:

1. What are the most important relationships in your company's strategy design links? During the LINKS process, you and your team discovered opportunities for your company. Those opportunities will demand stronger relationships between various individual links in the Strategic Value Chain. Map out, on paper, each of those links.

For example, assume you offer a service to business. You have determined that your company can greatly enhance your service with a voice response unit that allows customers 24-hour access to account information. In this case, technology and sales must be closely linked to provide effective service.

Perhaps you are marketing a product to mass merchandisers who now demand faster delivery and real time information on the status of orders. For your company to succeed, you must build strong links between product, distribution, marketing, sales, and customer service.

2. What measurements have you established and to what extent does each of these measurements correlate with profit and growth at the front line level? For example, if the marketing department has incorporated new processes for doing business, you must set up measurements that demonstrate whether your new processes are working and how well. Are you able to assess how well individuals and departments are producing? How do you measure the output of a department both qualitatively and quantitatively?

3. Is the importance of these relationships reflected in rewards and incentives offered to employees? Is the

relationship between rewards and achievement clear and fair? Do the rewards and incentives help management meet its goals?

4. How do you measure employee productivity? The effectiveness of sales is measured easily by units sold and profitability of sales. Manufacturing can be measured by profitability of units produced. Creating measurements is not always so easy or clear cut. For example, has the technology department installed software or hardware that affects speedier information that was previously lacking? As a result, are people able to make better decisions? That too is a measurement of success. Is your marketing department getting the word out and creating more customer-responsive marketing plans that are tied into new products or services?

Are your marketing and sales departments using information coming in through real time to database and get greater depth of content and feedback? Are they "data-mining" to get more information and a better understanding of the consumer/customer to further the reach and purchasing power of current clients and consumers?

Measure feedback from customer or consumer phone calls and correspondence to learn if you are doing the job. You must establish measurements for other areas of the company such as training, warehousing and shipping, and operations. When you have finished with all of these measures, you then turn to your top line. Is it growing? If so you are on the right track.

5. To what extent do measures of productivity identify changes in the quality as well as the quantity of service/product produced per units of input? If you failed to make a profit manufacturing 100 widgets last year, but are making a profit manufacturing 90 widgets this year, then you did something right. If you put $10 more into your services, but sales have gone down, you have not added value nor invested in your service properly. If, however, your sales have gone up exponentially, you have invested wisely.

■ Does the Culture Factor Contribute?

Ask yourself: To what extent is your company's leadership energetic and creative vs. stately and conservative? Certainly change comes more easily to a creative and energetic management team. While these are qualities to strive for, your company's culture cannot change overnight. Be realistic about how quickly you can affect changes based on the cultural mode.

Is the company's leadership participatory or distant, hands-on or hands-off? Can you afford to be distant or hands-off? If you are, do you have people in place who *are* participatory and hands-on?

Does the company's leadership operate in a listening, coaching, and teaching mode or a supervising and managing mode? Which mode will work better for you now? What do you have to do to switch to that style of leadership?

■ Communicating the Message

All your best ideas count for nothing if you and your team don't communicate your action plans to both your internal people and your customers or consumers. Each aspect of the plan, each link in your strategic assessment plan must first be communicated before it can be achieved. To facilitate your communications use the chart in Exhibit 22–1. In the first column, write in your action plan for each link. (Strategic Links that require similar communications, such as the vision and mission, have been grouped together.) Use the second column for internal communications plans and the third column to record external communications plans. While all changes must be communicated internally, some may not require external communications.

Let's look at ways to communicate your action plans for various links.

The Link	Action Plan	Internal Communications	External Communications
1. Vision 2. Mission-Objectives			
3. Corporate Culture 4. Infrastructure: Framework for the Future 5. The Organization			
6. Operations			
7. The New Consumerism 8. The New Marketing 9. Product/Service: Does It Still Fit? 10. Channel Power			
11. Real Time 12. Distribution: Right Time/Right Place			
13. Training: The Continuous Tool 14. The Top Line 15. Measurements for Success 16. Make It Happen!			

Exhibit 22–1
Communicating the Message

Vision/Mission

Internal:
- Should be available to everyone in the company.
- Print signs and post on bulletin boards.

External:
- Advertise vision and mission when appropriate.
- Incorporate into annual reports and promotional statements.

The Culture Factor

Internal: • Strong communications via key training meetings.
           • Prepare training modules incorporating culture, infrastructure, organization and operations.
           • Emphasize how departments will intercommunicate.

External: • Train your people to communicate differently.
           • Present new image and positioning through sales people, sales promotion, advertising, and public relations.

Infrastructure

Internal: • Communicate expectations and understanding of framework changes in training sessions.

External: • Advise sales, advertising, and public relations on key changes.
           • Assess whether customers must be contacted differently.
           • Sales people educate customers on changes to working relationship.
           • Advertising and public relations people communicate visuals to current and potential customers differently.

Organization

Internal: • Create an organization chart and distribute to key people.
           • Incorporate changes into training modules.
           • In smaller companies, discuss changes and incorporate into standard operating procedure (SOP) book.

Operations

Internal:
- Put all systems, controls, or procedural changes in writing.
- Set up meetings to explain changes.
- Train people to function within the new operations.

External:
- Contact customers affected by systems and policy changes.

The New Consumerism/The New Marketing/Product/Service Does It Still Fit?/Channel Power. These four Links are all about communications.

Internal:
- Communicate databasing, research, and focus group information throughout the company.
- Monitor each link's interdepartmental communications.

External:
- Ask how influx of information affects company's image and positioning.
- Communicate changes in products/services, channels of distribution, and marketing directions to customers and consumers with completely integrated marketing effort.

Real Time

Internal:
- Decide: how will information be disseminated, to whom?
- How will information be internalized, analyzed, or datamined?
- Who does information go to after datamining?

External
- How is information utilized to dialogue with customers differently?
- How will real time affect sales planning, business planning, and working with new customers?

Right Place/Right Time

Internal: • Communicate changes to distribution, sales, production, advertising, and customer service.
           • Train people in the demands of real time and affect on inventory, shipping.

External: • Communicate changes to customers via sales force.
           • Communicate with truckers, freight people, and others.
           • Hold dialogues with customer receiving departments.

Training. Training is communicating. Communicating change often involves training.

Internal: • Training works hand-in-hand with team on all changes.
           • Develops training modules for employees.

External: • Develops training modules for customers.

Top Line/Measurements for Success/Make It Happen

Internal: • Communicate importance of controls in actualizing change.
           • Communicate how controls work, what information they provide.

External: • Communicate great top line in annual reports, public relation releases.

Remember the medium is the message, and keep it simple, stupid (KISS)! Anything that is too cluttered doesn't work, so use one theme.

Now that you have mastered some important tactics, let's look at some of the other drivers of change such as brand equity and Cybertraks—those major trends that are significantly changing our world and your business.

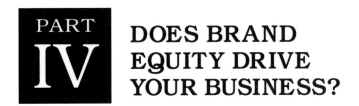

PART IV

DOES BRAND EQUITY DRIVE YOUR BUSINESS?

Okay, you assessed the links in your Strategic Value Chain in Part II and explored the tactics you will use to achieve your strategic objectives in Part III. Now let's take a look at your brands. Do you really have brands? If so, what's their value? If not, do you really need brands? Maybe not. Take this fast test and score your brand-ability.

1. Check which statement (honestly) best describes your current brand development position?
   - ❏ A. We see no need to change anything about our brands. If ain't broke, don't fix it.
   - ❏ B. Building brand equity is always on our agenda.
   - ❏ C. We review our brands every year.
   - ❏ D. We're not a branded company and shouldn't be. I am only reading these chapters because I want to keep current on everything that could affect my business.

2. We have definite plans to expand our branded line of products or services based on:
   - ❏ A. Our competition's recent expansion.
   - ❏ B. Results of our databasing efforts.
   - ❏ C. Sales figures.

3. The most essential element in building brand equity is:
   - ❏ A. A really hot logo.
   - ❏ B. A thorough understanding of consumer/customer demand.
   - ❏ C. Sufficient funds to mount a strong promotional campaign.

4. When growing equity through brand extension, the best place to start is with:
   - ❏ A. A collection of unrelated products or services that need a brand name to help them hang together.
   - ❏ B. A product or service that has the trust and loyalty of customers/consumers.
   - ❏ C. A product or service that is not widely known, but has a positive image among a limited group of customers.

5. The best result of building brand loyalty is:
   - ❏ A. You don't have to put as much into the product or service and can still charge a premium price.
   - ❏ B. Your company has a future.
   - ❏ C. Employees feel good about working for your company.

Scoring: Give yourself 20 points for each B answer, 10 points for each C, and 0 points for each A. If your answer to question 1 is D, give yourself an automatic 100 points.

100 points	Your brand ability is tops. Head for the 21st century.
80–90 points	Pretty good. Are you sure good is good enough? Learn more.

40–70 points	Your competition can sleep easy tonight. You, on the other hand, should stay up and finish the following chapters.
30 points or less	Have your ever thought about trading pork bellies?

Does your brand ability need a little polishing? Then read on. In Chapters 23 through 24, we will talk about analyzing brands, developing brand strategies, and building and evolving brand equity—all essential links in creating powerful brands that can drive your business into the future.

23

Brand Analysis and Strategy

Put Your Brand on the Couch

There is everything in a name. A rose by any other name would smell as sweet, but would not cost half as much during the winter months.

George Ade, journalist and humorist

George Ade probably wasn't thinking of brand names when he penned his pronouncement about the price of roses in winter, but it fits nonetheless. During both good times and lean times, plenty and scarcity, a trusted brand name is a company's best insurance policy. But, what is a *brand?* The *American Heritage Dictionary* defines a brand as "a trademark or distinctive name identifying a product or a manufacturer." Another definition for brand is "a name, symbol, or special design that identifies the products of one seller from those of others."

A *brand name* is words or letters that can be spoken. For example, Nabisco, IBM, Ford Taurus, Apple, and Federal Express are all brand names. A *brand mark,* on the other hand, is a symbol, design,

181

or distinctive lettering that is identifiable with a particular brand. Nike's swoosh symbol is a brand mark. So is that ornate daggerlike symbol that rock star Prince now uses to identify himself. A *trademark* is simply a brand for which a company has sought legal protection.

People are so familiar with mega-brands like Coca-Cola, Levi's, Hanes, and McDonald's, that they sometimes assume only giants can manage a brand. Not so. Brands can be regional, such as the Lettuce Entertain You restaurants in Chicago and ABC Carpet & Home in New York, or local, such as Miss MaryJane's Bakery Shop and Happy Returns Tax Service in Anywhere, U.S.A.

That doesn't mean that a company can create a brand simply by putting the company name on whatever product or service they sell. While a name on a product or service may differentiate it from the competitors' and take it out of the commodity realm, a name does not truly become a brand until your customers or consumers say so.

How do they say so? The true definition of a brand is always founded in consumer acceptance—a combination of brand awareness and loyalty. The value of a brand lies not just in its physical assets, but in a package of value-added intangibles that are validated by the customer or consumer each time they buy the product or service.

To achieve true brand status, a brand must be created, nurtured, and developed—strategically. That takes planning, work, and usually a substantial investment. For some companies, developing a brand may not be worth the effort. For other companies, brands are their most important assets.

Brands are usually built over long periods of time—one product or service at a time. New products evolve out of earlier products, services grows from original services. The growth of brand equity *must* be evolutionary if it is to make sense to the consumer. Ideally, a company's brand or family of brands will fit together cohesively within the company's structure. Unfortunately, even in a well-managed company brands may develop in a piecemeal manner. While a rationale existed for each product or service as it developed, chances are the end result is not a cohesive brand or family of brands, with each product or service meshing with the others. Sometimes you must step back and deconstruct what you have done previously and then reconstruct the pieces in order to create a more cohesive whole.

■ Get Fit

Let's illustrate this with an exercise called *Get Fit* that primes you and your team to look at new ways to create a cohesive brand package. For this exercise, you will be using L-shapes, such as the one in Exhibit 23–1. We will start with one L-shape, then add another. Later we will add two more L-shapes. Our objective is to fit the shapes together to create the most stable and most pleasingly designed geometric object possible with the pieces at hand. The L-shape represents a single-branded product. Whether you market a number of products under one brand or several brands in a family of brands, you want each to fit together as productively and efficiently as possible. This exercise can help show you how to get started.

You will need:

1. Paper.
2. Pencil.

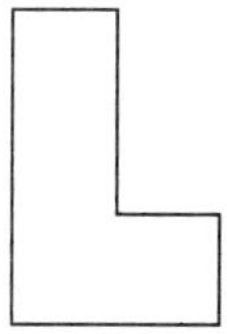

Exhibit 23–1
Get Fit: Campbell's Soup

Draw or trace the L-shape in Exhibit 23–1. This first L-shape represents a company's first product or service. In this case, we'll use the Campbell Soup Company as an example.

In 1897, the Campbell Soup Company discovered how to condense soup by removing most of the water. This technological discovery gave the company a competitive edge that pushed its brand—Campbell's Soup—to national prominence. The brand's identity was fortified with the introduction of the Campbell's Kids in 1904. Let's think of Campbell's Tomato Soup or Campbell's Chicken Noodle Soup as the first L-shape.

Many years later, Campbell Soup Company acquired V-8 juice—the second L-shape in their family of brands. (See Exhibit 23–2.) How would you draw this second L-shape to fit with the first? Try it. Chances are you created the design in Exhibit 23–3, by snuggling together the two L-shapes that represent your first two products or services. Finding synergies between your first two products or services, shouldn't be difficult, if your brand development is evolutionary rather than revolutionary.

Years pass. New technology comes along and suggests ideas for new branded products and services. For Campbell Soup Company, through acquisition and development, those brands included Swanson, Vlasic, Mrs. Paul's, Godiva Chocolatier, Prego, and LeMenu frozen dinners, among many others.

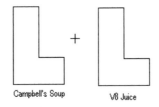

Exhibit 23–2
Get Fit: Campbell's Soup + V-8

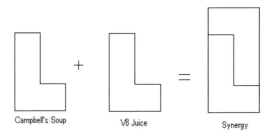

Exhibit 23–3
Get Fit: Synergy

Now you have at least two more L-shapes to add to your previous design as in Exhibit 23–4. How will you add these to form a cohesive whole? Give it a try. Most people will simply repeat what they did previously. They will again nestle the two new shapes together, then stack them end-to-end or side-by-side as in Exhibits 23–5 and 23–6. What kind of whole do they make? Is this really the best you can do?

Not if you "think out of the box" and decide to deconstruct the relationship of the first two L-shapes. If you begin to look at the 4 L-shapes as individual pieces to be assembled in a completely new pattern, you may create Exhibit 23–7—a more cohesive and stronger design. So too you must look at each of the products or services that constitute your brand or family of brands. How can they best fit to create greater brand equity for your company? (See Exhibit 23–8.)

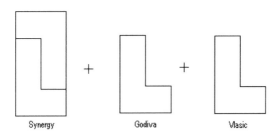

Exhibit 23–4
Get Fit: Synergy + Godiva + Vlasic

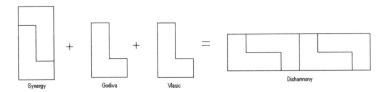

Exhibit 23–5
Get Fit: Disharmony

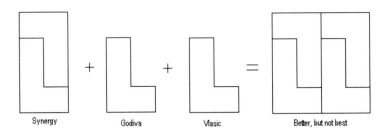

Exhibit 23–6
Get Fit: Better, But Not Best

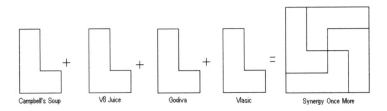

Exhibit 23–7
Get Fit: Synergy Once More

The Top Line.   As your company, your products or services, and your brands grow and evolve, they must be monitored constantly. Do each of your brands or products and services within your brand still belong in your company? Would selling or spinning off a brand better serve both the brand and your company? Does each really fit within your image or

Exhibit 23-8
Get Fit

your new strategic direction? Is it time for reassessment and realignment?

That is what most companies eventually find necessary. Even the global and highly successful Campbell's has done a little re-engineering, selling off noncore businesses, such as Mallow Foods, Campbell Chilled Foods, Laforest Perigord, and Win Schuler cheeses. It has recently restructured itself and acquired the Erasco Group, Germany's leader in soups and canned meals, in its effort to become a giant in the global market. Be aware that as you build brand equity, you may have to step back and analyze each piece of your equity and how those pieces fit.

■ To Brand or Not to Brand

Brands are not essential for success. There are pros and cons. Why brand? Branding a product can benefit both company and customer. For the company, branding:

- Identifies a product or service.
- Facilitates advertising.
- Helps producers, service providers, or retailers control the market by eliminating. confusion about various products.
- Reduces price competition by differentiating products.
- Adds prestige to what would ordinarily be commodity items. (Consider Morton's salt or Purdue chicken.)
- Stimulates customers to pay more for the brand's added value.

From the customer or consumer point-of-view, branding:

- Assures a level of quality.
- Promises consistency and reliability.
- Conveys status.
- Saves shopping time.
- Assures a certain price level.

Those are all things you want, right? Not so fast. There are still a few good reasons not to brand. Don't brand if:

- You are unable or unwilling to promote the brand. A brand *must* be properly marketed and promoted; but doing so may not be worth the expense and time.

- You cannot maintain consistent quality. The idea behind a brand is to assure the customer that his expectations will be met consistently. If you cannot do that, branding is self-defeating.

■ Analyzing Your Brands' Equity

A brand is a powerful package of intangibles. Brand equity can't be seen, touched, felt or tasted, but you know when it's there. It doesn't show up on your balance sheet or in your inventory, but it may be your single most valuable asset. Coca-Cola, Nike, Levi Strauss & Co., Campbell's, and IBM, for example, have each built a strong image in the public consciousness through careful planning and execution of product, pricing, promotion, advertising, and distribution strategies. Take away these marketers' manufacturing facilities, sales organizations, inventory, and other tangibles, and they would still retain a very valuable asset—the equity of their brand name supported by their brand image. According to *Financial World*'s 1995 brand survey, Coca-Cola, with annual sales of approximately $16 billion, is the world's most valuable brand, worth a staggering $39 billion. (To estimate the value of various brands, the magazine used a complicated formula which involves calculating the operating income and net income and assigning a multiple based on such criteria as leadership, stability, market strength, global prospects, and communications strength.) What would the company be worth today, if it had chosen not to brand? It certainly wouldn't be a global giant with a brand known to nearly every human being on earth.

A brand name can be a precious asset; but it's also a perishable asset, which must be protected and nurtured throughout a constant state of evolution. A wide range of problems can beset a brand name that is not properly protected. Consider the brand name that has fallen into generic use. Linoleum, celluloid, kerosene, aspirin, and shredded wheat were all once brand names, not generic designations. These former brand names, however, became household words and were so identified with their respective products that they lost their brand identity.

A brand's equity, which is based on a combination of brand awareness and brand loyalty, must be protected constantly. A company cannot afford to have it tarnished. Think of the many brands that have been severely harmed by product tampering, liability suits, and calamities (such as the Dow silicone breast implants). While such events can severely damage, or even destroy, a brand, at least the company involved knows it has a problem and is compelled to act.

A more likely scenario is brand dilution, which can affect any business with a name to protect, whether it's a manufacturer's brand, a license or a store name, or whether it's globally, nationally, regionally, or locally recognized. Brand erosion usually affects companies that are not following the precepts of the New Consumerism and the New Marketing. If you are listening to your customer or consumer on a daily basis, you will know whether your brand's equity is slipping and what you should do about it.

How can you tell if your brand name is losing its luster? Answer honestly.

- Does your product no longer demand full price regularly?
- Are private label products eating away at your sales?
- Are you consistently cutting prices to meet low cost competition?
- Are your traditional marketing tools—advertising and promotion—no longer effective?

If you answer yes to any of these questions, then be aware that the consumer is letting you know your brand has lost at least some of its value. You've got *brand erosion!*

When a brand's sales slip, too many executives resort to outdated responses, such as cost-cutting, short-term price cuts, and other sales gimmicks that only provide short-term sales increases. Cutting prices only erodes brand equity further, eventually turning the product into a commodity.

Instead of cutting prices, companies must apply New Marketing principles. That means targeting and meeting consumer needs quickly by integrating quick response into the company's manufacturing and marketing capabilities. The key to successful brand development, whether it's building a new brand or reviving an old one, is to marry consumer demand to company assets. The marketer must determine what those assets are, then devise strategies that best utilize those assets. Calvin Klein's creation of cK one fragrance for men and women is a prime example. The company lent its expertise in fragrances to a product for a young, unisex market and captured a very broad audience. Virgin Atlantic, to entice the first-class customer who travels frequently, created Upper Class for the price of first class. Travelers can be manicured, pedicured, and massaged in the Upper Class club prior to boarding. And on-board each passenger has a choice of films to view on his own personal monitor.

During brand analysis, you and your team will go through many of the same steps that you did during product assessment. You will seek to learn more about all the processes involved in product development, promotion, and advertising. You will examine your supply chain performance. And you will also seek to understand your consumers' buying patterns and their assessment of your brand's equity. The objective of this analysis is not just to understand your existing brand as completely as possible, but also to determine what brand extensions or additions your customers want and need and whether your current capabilities can accommodate these. If you were to introduce a luxury version of your brand's product or service, is your current supply chain adequate for the job? Would your customers or consumers welcome new products or services brought out under the umbrella of your brand name? If you are producing a product, could your current manufacturing or sourcing accommodate brand extensions?

Begin by objectively examining all your company's capabilities from manufacturing resources and product knowledge through personnel and distribution channels. To what extent can you adapt those assets to meet changing demands? Be very much aware of your company's financial capabilities too. Finances often determine how fast and how far you can take a brand.

■   Plotting Your Brand's Course

Once you have analyzed your brands and understand your consumers' or customers' attitudes toward them, you are ready to plot out a brand strategy. What are the options available to you?

If you are a manufacturer, a consumer products company, or a service provider you have a number of choices.

- *Market your entire product or service output under your own brand.* Are you a large, well-financed company with broad product lines? Do you have well-established distribution systems that are working for you? Do you have substantial market share? Then you may want to proceed like IBM and market all your products under your own brand name.

- *Brand fabricated parts and materials.* This is an option available to both manufacturers and service providers. Do you make products bought for replacement purposes? Does your product or service lend prestige to the offering? Do you have more resources to advertise and promote than the company which uses your components? Then you may want to follow the lead DuPont's Dacron polyester. Or like Intel, let the consumer know that it's an Intel Pentium chip inside that computer to add luster to the finished product.

- *Market under a licensed name.* Whether it's an organization such as NFL, NHL, or Major League Baseball
  or an individual such as Elizabeth Taylor's White Di-
  amonds and Black Pearls fragrances, licensed names
  can give instant brand recognition and cache to an
  otherwise unknown company. Be aware, however, that
  you have far less control over a licensed name, which
  can tarnish and erode as easily as any company-
  owned brand. The baseball strike of 1994, for example,
  did little for the sale of Major League Baseball merchandise. There are no guarantees in branding.

Strategically a retailer might choose to:

- *Develop the store brand.* Whether you are creating private label merchandise or building the equity of your
  store's name, a retailer must consider developing its
  own brand equity to leverage its way into the future.
  Consider ABC Carpet & Home in New York City, a store
  that started as a push cart and developed into a home
  furnishings phenomenon with cache and brand equity
  that stretch far beyond the city limits. What are the
  value and equity of such brands? That depends on the
  reach of your operation. It could be local, regional, national, or global. A store's brand equity may stretch
  across county or state lines. It may include entire sections of the country or, like Bloomingdale's, Gucci's,
  and Tiffany's, it may have global cache. Your brand
  equity may allow you to go on-line within your trading
  area or nationally and even internationally.
    Developing your store name as a brand can pro-
  vide benefits that will lead your company into the 21st
  century. As a retailer, do you want to increase control
  over the market? Your own brand achieves this since
  the customer can only access it through your operation. Do you want more freedom in pricing and the
  ability to differentiate your products from those of the

competition? If you control the production of merchandise, you can price your brands below national
brands and still make a higher profit. Developing your
own brand equity will go a long way to assuring a dif-
ferentiated product and greater freedom in pricing.

Some strategies are common to all companies, whether
service, business-to-business, or manufacturer:

- *Branding an entire line of products under one name.*
  Heinz and Federal Express, for example, use a family
  blanket brand for their products and services. Are all
  your products related in quality and usage? Then a
  blanket brand may work for you. Prestige is spread out
  and introducing new products is simpler and less expensive than bringing out entirely new brands.
- *Using a separate name for each product.* Procter and
  Gamble does it. So do many other consumer products
  companies.
- *Applying a separate family brand to each grade of product or service or each group of similar offerings.* Consider Estee Lauder, which successfully launched
  Origins, a cosmetic line that presents a very different
  image than that of the Lauder brand.

Whichever strategy or combination of strategies you
choose, it should relate to your vision, mission, and objectives. Your branding decisions should also be rooted in
consumer/customer information gathered through New Marketing techniques, such as databasing. Ask too if your
strategies offer your brands and your company a future. Seriously consider whether your system of branding is outdated. Does it keep you bound to the past or does it help you
to continuously build brand equity?

24

Brand Equity Builders

Put $$$ in Your Piggy Bank

Things are only worth what you make them worth.
Moliere, *Les Precieuses Ridicules*

What builds a brand's equity? How can you measure it and how can you grow it? Start with the understanding that brand equity is added value, the value that goes beyond the physical assets of the product or service. How do we quantify that? First, let's look at the pieces that create equity.

Performance gives value. Does your product or service perform consistently? Brand equity is forged with consumers or customers over time. Do your brands have longevity? Symbolically do they represent integrity to the consumer? Do your customers or consumers demonstrate brand loyalty by purchasing and repurchasing? The consumer's positive perception of a brand controls the positive equity of that brand, while erosion of consumer commitment equals a decline in equity.

Another key to developing brand equity lies in building upon improvements you make in your operations. If you can link these improvements to brand equity, you will inevitably improve your brand's profitability. Any technological development that speeds your product or service to market or improves your customer or consumer contact will create greater brand equity and value.

How do you measure equity?

- *Monitor purchasing behavior.* Again, you must apply New Consumerism and New Marketing principles and listen to the customer. What is the consumer or customer telling you he or she wants to buy? Are the channels of communications open and are you listening? Next, what is your customer actually buying? How does that behavior compare with purchasing behavior in previous years, months, or weeks? How has purchasing behavior changed in relation to competitive products? Are changes in purchasing behavior related solely to brand image and equity or are the changes the result of other influences? For example, is new technology making your product or service obsolete? Is the economy impacting your brand's sales?

- *Monitor the level of customer or consumer commitment so you can anticipate market changes and formulate marketing strategies.* Is the customer truly committed and loyal or is your product or service simply the best choice available at the moment?

As W. Edwards Deming states in *Out of the Crisis*, "Committed customers enhance the value of a brand in many ways." He goes on to cite those ways:

- By resisting competitor's discounting.
- Reducing market costs.
- Providing a source of consistent demand.
- Providing time to respond to competitive threats.

- Encouraging and convincing others to buy.
- By providing a ready market for brand extensions.

Although brand equity is intangible, it can be measured in various ways. Brand equity is based on a combination of brand awareness and brand loyalty. Strong loyalty and widespread awareness equal powerful brand equity. Brands can be placed into four categories depending on the relative levels of loyalty and awareness. Using the Brand Power Pyramid shown in Exhibits 24–1 and 24–2, brands can be classified as:

1. *Power brands.* Brands with high levels of awareness and loyalty; these are the brands with national or global reach.
2. *Niche brands.* These brands enjoy high loyalty levels but relatively low awareness levels. Frequently the brand names of luxury products or services or those

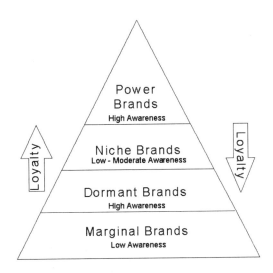

Exhibit 24–1
Brand Power Pyramid

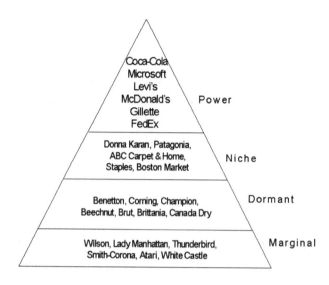

Exhibit 24–2
Brands in Power

of companies serving local or regional markets are
niche brands.

3. *Dormant brands.* These are brands which are relative
   well-known but have lower levels of consumer loyalty.
   With attention to consumer or customer feedback they
   are ripe for revival.

4. *Marginal brands.* General these brands have low loyalty and low or limited awareness. These may be
   brands that are in decline or simply brand names that
   have never been properly nurtured.

Where in this pyramid does your brand fall? And in what
direction is it moving? Brand equity is dynamic with consumer perception changing constantly. You can only stay
current with those changes if you are in continuous contact
with your consumer or customer. Then you will be aware of
your brand's constant evolution. How you work to control
that evolution can make all the difference between making
your way into the 21st century or becoming a relic.

■ Equity Evolution: Getting Your Brand from Here to There

Your brands *must* change to stay vital and profitable, but you must keep those changes *evolutionary, not revolutionary.* Like the manufacturer of lawn furniture who decides he wants to produce television sets, if you attempt revolutionary changes, the customer won't buy it. Change must be consistent with the image and the product or service you offer.

But within that framework, you and your management team have room for experimentation and originality. You can try to shape your brand equity in the easiest, fastest way or you can act strategically and create brand equity that stretches in new directions.

■ Building Equity through Brand Extension

One logical approach to building equity is brand extension— adding on modified products or services to meet the changing demands of your customer or to better target the needs of a particular market segment or particle. Consider how some products have evolved over the last few decades. Ice cream, for example, isn't the same product we enjoyed as kids. Remember going to the store for Sealtest ice cream? It was either vanilla, strawberry, chocolate, or some combination of these flavors. It came in half gallon boxes and cost about $1.59. Today we can enjoy all kinds of ice creams and variations on ice creams, including designer ice creams, such as Ben and Jerry's, and ice creams with foreign accents, such as Haagen Dazs. We have fancy flavors from Heathbar and chocolate chip cookie to praline and cream de menthe. We can have mango, cappuccino, key lime, and kiwi. Chocolate isn't just chocolate anymore. Now you can choose from fudge swirl, Dutch chocolate, brownie fudge chocolate, and chocolate chocolate chip to name a few. If those don't fit your dietary requirements, there's fat-free ice cream, sugar-free ice cream, ice milk, sorbet and sherbet, and a host of other "diet lites." Frozen yogurt is available in fat-free and sugar-free varieties. Or there's nondairy for the lactose intolerant. Of course, instead of paying $1.59 a half gallon, you're paying $3.19 for a pint and $2.00 for a single dip cone.

How did this happen? Like all solid product and brand developments it occurred gradually. The frozen dessert folks developed niche markets, moved into new areas and strategically planned step-by-step for the future by understanding who their customers were, what they wanted, and how those wants continued to change over the years.

Spaghetti was considered exotic in the early days of the 20th century, when it was introduced to the United States. Over the years, it developed into a staple of the American diet, and not a very exciting one at that. Companies such as Ronzoni sold their spaghetti at 69 cents a box. Ten years ago, spaghetti didn't look like a hot marketing category. But the folks at Ronzoni and other companies discovered the potential of brand-equity evolution. They began extending their brands by introducing the American consumer to other forms of "pasta." Linguine, fettucini, angel hair, bow ties, ziti, and dozens of other shapes and colors took their places on grocery shelves. Sauces were a natural extension of this business. Sauce with sausage, marinara sauce, and vegetarian joined traditional spaghetti sauce on the shelves. The producers took a commodity product and turned it into a fashion food. Now marketers have extended the category further by offering fresh pastas, such as fettucini and ravioli, along with pesto and Alfredo sauces in the refrigerated section of the supermarket. The 69-cent box of spaghetti has moved in strategic directions. Today we are willing to spend $4.99 to $6.99 for fresh sauce and pasta.

Marketers such as Ronzoni evolved their brands by adding new products and moving to complementary products. In the sporting goods industry, Spalding took a similar path to strategically building brand equity. Remember the little rubber Spalding ball that cost 25 cents? Today the

Spalding name is connected to many sports products and carries with it tremendous equity.

Athletic shoe marketers have worked strategically by developing the product category itself to meet the needs of many segments of the market. You remember the old-fashioned sneaker. The male version was a black, high top; the ladies wore white canvas styles that cost $5.99. These once-inexpensive footwear products (don't call them sneakers anymore) have moved in new strategic directions. They are now "athletic shoes" and cost from $50 to $150 or more a pair. Today you can buy athletic shoes designed for walking, cross training, jogging, running, tennis, basketball, and just about any other sport you can imagine. You can even pump them and blow them up. The footwear people niche marketed and strategically directed the old sneaker into a huge market. Today the names Nike and Reebok are among the best known in the world. This didn't happen by accident; it was all *evolutionary*, not *revolutionary*.

Branded services evolve, too. Even the much maligned U.S. Postal Service has used consumer feedback to change its offerings. Once we had regular mail, Parcel Post, and air mail. Technology, competition, and consumer demand has forced the Post Office to offer guaranteed overnight Express Mail and Priority Mail. Of course, you are paying $3 to $20 for these special services, rather than a few cents.

Over the last decade, we have niche marketed and grown our products, services, and brand names through strategic marketing efforts and an understanding of the various components involved in moving a brand along. None of this can be based on guess work. New Marketing methodologies must be in place providing, through databasing and datamining the critical information needed to move forward.

■ Break the Rules

How can you start the evolutionary process rolling? Before you begin, let's do one more mental aerobic exercise to keep you thinking out of the box. I call it *The Rule Breaker.* Its purpose is to demonstrate that most of the rules are in your head. You have to break those rules to keep your mind open to fresh approaches to brand equity extension.

You will need:

1. Paper.
2. Pencil.

Draw nine dots like those in Exhibit 24–3. Now, link all of the dots with four continuous straight lines. Draw the lines without lifting your pencil from the paper. It sounds easy, until you start. If you think it can't be done, ask yourself if you are trying to follow self-imposed rules. When you're ready to look at the solution, turn to Exhibit 24–4 on page 204.

The Top Line.   This is really thinking out of the box. Did you assume that you couldn't draw your lines beyond the box or outside the perimeter of the dots? Whose rules were those? If you are going to build your brand equity, you will have to put aside self-limiting assumptions and keep your mind open to new ideas and creative solutions.

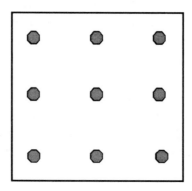

Exhibit 24–3
Box the Dots

Start the Evolution Now!

Now let's start applying this to your products and services. Again, gather your strategic assessment team. Using consumer/customer data and other information you have gathered during brand analysis, discuss the evolutionary possibilities of each branded product. If you have a small team, five or fewer, begin by assigning one question to each member. If your assessment team is larger, have members work in pairs.

1. *How can you modify your branded product or service to appeal to a new group of consumers?* For example, if your branded product or service appeals mostly to men, such as razors and razor blades, how can it be modified to appeal to women? How can it be modified to appeal to a different age group? Think of the pros and cons.

2. *How can you effect economies in your branded product or services—while maintaining quality and image—in order to appeal to a wider market?*

3. *How can your branded product or service be modified so that you can sell more to your current customers?* For example, if your company sells food products through consumer catalogues, can you entice customers to buy more by offering new assortments or promoting the gift-giving potential of your brand?

4. *How can new technology affect your brand's evolution?* Can it help differentiate your product or service as it has the tennis racket? Or can technology change your product or service more profoundly? Think of the evolution of the computer from a numbers cruncher for business to a communications and design tool for home and business. Think of how technology continues to create new services for telephone companies. How can your brand evolve and grow along with technology?

5. *Can you extend your brand equity by building a family of related products and services?* For example, if you offer

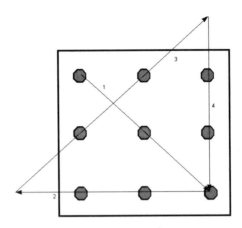

Exhibit 24–4
Break the Rules

life insurance, can your trusted brand name carry your company into home owner's insurance or automobile insurance? Or like the spaghetti producers, can you move into new, but related, products?

Instruct your team members not to be concerned with current manufacturing or sourcing restrictions, supply chain limitations, or financial restraints. At this stage, they should use a "thinking out of the box" approach and focus only on the brand, its equity, and how to evolve it. Your team members should have open access to all the company's consumer data, research, and other information. Set a time limit. Then ask each member or pair of members to make an oral presentation.

Where can this lead? Where can brand evolution take your company? To a new vision, greater brand equity, a change in consumer expectations about your brand and its competitive space, to greater consumer loyalty, and new consumers.

PART V

CYBERTRAKS

The new electronic interdependence recreates the world in the image of a global village.

Marshall McLuhan, *The Gutenberg Galaxy*

Marshall McLuhan prophesied the electronic age. When McLuhan wrote about the creation of a global village, he envisioned a world connected by the powerful, unifying message of television. But his vision applies as well, if not better, to cyberspace, the global economy, and all the other cybertraks leading us into the next millennium.

Cybertraks are those major demographic, social, and technological trends that offer opportunities for change and growth as you move into the next millennium. You need to understand how these trends will affect the way you do business in the future and how you can best take advantage of them to spur your company's growth.

In the following four chapters we will explore key cybertraks: the Aging of America, Ethnic Diversity, the Echo Boom, the Information Culture, the Educational Imperative, the Ecological Movement, Health Awareness, and Homing— the growing importance of the home as the center of both personal and professional life. Other cybertraks, which we cover in Chapters 26 through 28, are Electronic Commerce, the Virtual Office, and Globalization. A few additional cybertraks that will lead us into the next century are shown on the art on page 206.

	1990	2000	2010	2020	2030	2040	2050	BEYOND
Consumer Trends	Consumer Trends Must Be Monitored Throughout Time							
Electronic Commerce		Early Starts Win						
Global Economy	Window Will Close!							
The Virtual Office		Stay Current, Change Is Constant						
Car of the Future			Just in Time to Spare Fossil Fuel Depletion					
Mach 2 Jet Travel			Only 45 Minutes to Tokyo!					
Ultimate Diet Pill		Get Ready for a Brave New Diet World						
Outer Space Real Estate					Lunar Condo, 5 Modules, Earth Vu			

Exhibit V–1
Cybertraks: Windows of Opportunity

In learning about these cybertraks, you will look for *LinkStrats,* or Linking Strategies—those points where a cybertrak conjoins with your company's products or services. Sometimes, the LinkStrat that links your company to a major cybertrak pre-exists. For example, the Aging of America is a major cybertrak. If you are a provider of geriatric health services, your LinkStrat is obvious. Just be certain that you are attuned to the changing mature market. If, however, you are a travel agent, you may have to adapt your services to fit the new mature market. In other words, you may have to create your own LinkStrat. In other cases, the cybertrak will have no relation to your business. If, for example, you produce industrial cleaning supplies, the Aging of America is not likely to be relevant to your sales.

The art on page 207 shows that a cybertrak, such as Diversity or Homing, links into your company's products or services through a LinkStrat—the linking strategy that you and your team will discover or create. The synergy of the cybertrak, your company, and the LinkStrat work to create new markets and increase sales and profits.

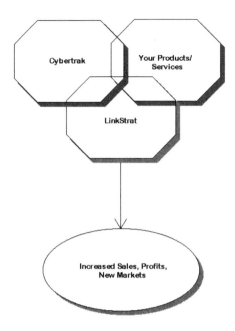

Exhibit V–2
LinkStrats = Sales + Profits + New Markets

In Chapter 3 you used the LINKS (Leverage Ideas to Navigate Key Strategies) process to find new opportunities for your company. To find the LinkStrats that effectively connect your company's products and services to key trends, you will again use this process. As you read the chapters ahead, remember that your future lies within these cybertraks. Many, if not all of them, will directly affect your business. They offer a bright, exciting future if, in fact, you do "leverage your ideas to navigate key strategies."

25

Consumer Trends

Cybertraks to the Future

Men and melons are hard to know.

Benjamin Franklin,
Poor Richard's Almanac

If Ben Franklin thought folks were hard to figure out back in the 1700s, what would he think now, given the diversity of our society? What about you? Think you have a pretty clear picture of today's consumer? Try this quick test to find out how accurate your ideas are. Check off the one correct answer.

Who Are We?

1. Which of the following types of households is most prevalent in the United States today?
   - ❏ A. Married couples with children.
   - ❏ B. Married couples without children.
   - ❏ C. Other families (including single mothers or fathers) with children.

2. If you want to sell the mature market, which of the following groups of states offers the best market? (More than 15 percent of the population is age 65 and older.)
    - ❏ A. Pennsylvania, North Dakota, Missouri, and Nebraska.
    - ❏ B. New Hampshire, Utah, North Carolina, and South Carolina.
    - ❏ C. Maine, Rhode Island, Alabama, and Ohio.

3. The state that experienced the greatest population growth from 1980 to 1990 is:
    - ❏ A. Florida.
    - ❏ B. Alaska.
    - ❏ C. Nevada.

4. Which race or ethnicity is the fastest growing segment of the U.S. population?
    - ❏ A. African-American.
    - ❏ B. Mexican.
    - ❏ C. Vietnamese.

5. What percentage of African-American households earn more than $50,000 a year?
    - ❏ A. 11%
    - ❏ B. 7%
    - ❏ C. 15%

6. What most frightens baby boomers?
    - ❏ A. The Internet.
    - ❏ B. Getting older.
    - ❏ C. Having too little money for retirement.

7. What's the most popular sport among affluent consumers?
    - ❏ A. Fitness walking.
    - ❏ B. Golf.
    - ❏ C. Polo.

8. Which ethnic group shops most frequently?
   - ❑ A. Asian-Americans.
   - ❑ B. Hispanics.
   - ❑ C. Irish-Americans.

Scoring: The answers are: 1. B., 2. A., 3. C., 4. C., 5. C., 6. C., 7. A., 8. A. According to the 1990 U.S. Census, Mendelsohn Affluent Survey, Municipal Bond Investors Assurance Corp., and MSR Ethnic Market Research, those are some of the surprising facts about the American consumer. How did you do?

Consumers have changed drastically in the last decade. Diversity and demassing have created particle markets and particles of particles, offering businesses new challenges and opportunities to find LinkStrats that connect their products and services to important consumer cybertraks.

Back when the baby boom was developing into the biggest cybertrak of all time, marketers viewed American consumers as relatively homogeneous. A family unit was white, middle to upper-middle class, with a male head-of-household, a housewife, and 2.5 children. It was the era of the mass market.

African-Americans, Hispanics, and other minorities were considered marginal consumers, targets for food products, or cigarettes at best. The gay market? Who knew? Senior citizens? Why bother? Today, with ever-increasing diversity and the demassing of markets, we can no longer afford to ignore any segment of the population. Nor can we continue to see consumer segments as one-dimensional. The Hispanic, African-American, or Asian market, for example, can no longer be treated as single entities. If you are marketing to an African-American male, did he come of age during Watergate or World War II? Does he live in the South or on the West Coast, in a major city or a small town? Is he college educated or a high school drop out, a doctor or a postal worker? Is he married? With children? Is he gay?

Recognizing consumers' many facets and the multiple roles each plays is a major precept of *particle marketing*. This concept recognizes that broad brush strokes are no longer adequate for creating a true picture of the consumer. Instead we must look for particles, particles of particles, and particles that intercept with other particles. Let's take another look at our African-American male. Assume he is a graduate of UCLA, a plastic surgeon working in Chicago, and is gay. Those facts present at least five particles and five points of approach for reaching this consumer.

In constructing portraits of consumers and consumer cybertraks, we must always be aware that trends cross over other trends and layer over the demographics of gender, ethnicity, class, income, education, and generational experiences. Let's look at some major consumer-related cybertraks.

- *The aging of America.* The United States, like other developed countries, is aging. Today, close to 65 million Americans are 50 or older. And watch out, because here come the 81 million baby boomers, who officially began turning 50 on New Year's Day 1996. Even without the boomers, it's a formidable market. Older consumers own 77 percent of all U.S. financial assets and 80 percent of the money in savings and loans. More than 77 percent own their own homes, many of which are mortgage free. Their children have finished college and are out on their own. As empty nesters, they have leisure time and the financial resources to enjoy it. The financial clout of this market will continue to grow with the inclusion of the baby boomers. But baby boomers will bring a new twist to marketing to mature adults. Just as baby boomers redefined youth in the 1960s, they will redefine maturity in the 1990s. Magazines such as *Modern Maturity* and *New Choices* are being redesigned to appeal to boomers. Marketers who target the older consumer cannot expect old marketing methods to succeed with graying boomers, who are better educated, more independent, more involved in activities, and healthier than previous generations.

- *The Millennium or Echo Generation.* 72 million children will come of age during the early years of the new Millennium. What can we expect from this group? According to the Census Bureau, 27 percent of the Millennium Generation are from one parent homes, compared with 12 percent of children in 1970. Only 67 percent are white, compared with 75 percent of the baby boomers. The first generation to grow up with computers, they may also become the first generation divided into technological haves and have-nots. Today's children and teens and tomorrow's young adults, they are media savvy, accustomed to diversity and alternative lifestyles. Their sheer numbers will force marketers to give them the same respect paid to boomers.

- *Diversity: Ethnic and otherwise.* Diversity cuts across generations as well as income and gender. Though the United States has been multicultural since its earliest days, most of those cultures were quickly assimilated because of one common denominator—color. Today the United States is changing colors, adding many shades of brown.

    According to U.S. Census figures, between 1980 and 1990, the overall population of the U.S. increased 9.8 percent. Broken down by race, the increases were: white, 6 percent; African-American, 13.2 percent; Native American, Eskimo, and Aleut Islanders, 37.9 percent; Asian or Pacific Islanders, 107.8 percent; Hispanic, 53 percent. These numbers reflect a trend going back over 30 years. Just over 80 percent of the population reporting in the 1990 Census considered itself white. That percentage will drop steadily throughout the next century.

As diversity intensifies, marketers will need to address each of these segments and the particles within these segments. Hispanics, for example, include Mexicans, Puerto Ricans, Cubans, Dominicans, and a host of South and Central American cultures as well as Spaniards. To effectively reach each of these distinct particles, marketers must understand their lifestyles and cultural backgrounds.

Marketers must also ask themselves how cultural and ethnic diversity changes the way people buy. How does it affect choices in apparel, foods, health and beauty products, cooking paraphernalia, home furnishings, appliances, and electronics? Who within the family purchases and who influences the purchase? Even the most sophisticated consumer products company must go to back to ground zero and investigate these questions.

Add in *gender diversity* as women continue to take on new roles throughout our society. While most marketers think they are old pros at addressing women, their expertise is usually limited to selling fashion, home products, and foods. Today women buy cars, securities, business and industrial products, and everything else. Marketers need to learn a lot more about how the other half thinks.

Finally, factor in the gay and lesbian market. Ten years ago, few marketers would have tried to capture this often affluent market. It's time for rethinking. Many gays and lesbians are well educated, hold high-paying jobs, and—with their lack of dependents—enjoy high levels of discretionary income. With the growth of the Gay Pride movement and more open acknowledgment of sexuality, this population has become more easily identified. Marketers who look to find LinkStrats with gays and lesbians should recognize this is not a homogeneous market. Gay and lesbian consumers come in all ages, races, and political persuasions.

Because gays and lesbians have traditionally been ignored by Corporate America, companies that go after this market intelligently often develop an extremely loyal customer. AT&T, Continental Airlines, Visa, and Absolut Vodka sponsored the 1994 Gay Games IV with success and apparently little backlash.

* *The Education Imperative.* The level of education has risen dramatically over the last 50 years for all segments of the population. In 1940 less than 25 percent of the population completed high school and less than 5 percent completed four or more years of college. This compares with a nearly 78 percent high school completion rate and over 21 percent college completion today. This holds true for all ethnic groups. Only 7.3 percent of African-Americans, for example, completed high school in 1940, compared with 66.2 percent today. College completion for African-Americans increased from 1.3 percent to 11.3 percent over the same period.

   While an education no longer guarantees a good job or high income, without a high school diploma— at minimum—the average young person can expect little more than a lifetime of marginal employment. Education becomes essential as technology and the Information Age take hold. Many question the ability of the public school system to provide relevant educations, and the real possibility exists that we may be dividing into a society of technological haves and have-nots.

   How can business capitalize? First, recognize that today's consumer is better educated and equipped to make intelligent buying decisions. Tremendous opportunities exist for educational institutions and training facilities that can provide the skills needed to compete in tomorrow's world. Finding new and less expensive ways to bring education and training to consumers should be an important goal.

- *Ecology.* Consumers are deeply aware of the damage done to the ecology in the United States and other countries. The Echo Generation is especially concerned about the world they are inheriting. Businesses must institute meaningful conservation and recycling programs wherever appropriate. The next generation will hold marketers more accountable for their actions. Products that promote a cleaner environment will also find markets.

- *Health.* America is obsessed with good health. We may not always do the right thing, but we know we should exercise at least three times a week, watch our fat intake, drink decaf, and take our antioxidant vitamins. The growth of HMOs, the ongoing campaign against cigarette smoking, and a refusal to accept the idea that aging and poor health are synonymous, have made Americans more aware of prevention. Factor in interest in holistic medicine and scepticism of traditional medicine for an added twist. The implications for business seem endless. Producers of food products and supplements, health care providers, exercise facilities, sporting goods retailers, and many others can key into this important cybertrak.

- *Homing.* With the development of the information culture, more corporations allow and encourage employees to work from their homes. The growth of entrepreneurial, home-based businesses adds fuel. As our homes become self-sufficient units, business opportunities arise for everyone from interiors designers and business equipment dealers to supermarkets that deliver on-line orders.

These are a few of the cybertraks leading us into the 21st century. To understand how to better interpret these trends, we must factor in the consumer's life stage and other demographics.

■ Generational Marketing: Keying into Life Experiences

Generational Marketing, marketing's new tool to connect with consumers, classifies consumers, not by age ranges, but by meaningful coming-of-age experiences. Generational Marketing says, for example, that those who came of age during the Depression—*Depression cohorts*—are uniquely branded by their experiences and react to the marketplace based on those experiences. While Generational Marketing still recognizes that actual age does affect market behavior. (A baby boomer who spent half her salary on Beatles albums at age 18, has different priorities at age 50.) It says we are foolish to expect the 50-year-old *baby boomer cohort* to behave as the Depression Cohort did at age 50. Generational Marketing provides an increasingly popular perspective on the New Consumerism. It offers a starting point for better understanding today's consumer trends. Advocates of Generational Marketing segment the adult population into the following six cohorts:

- *Depression cohorts,* born 1912–1921, were defined by the Depression. Marketers must remember that this group values security and seldom spends freely.
- *World War II cohorts,* born 1922–1927. The sacrifices of World War II and faith in a common goal were their shared experiences. They are brand loyal and spend carefully.

- *Post war cohorts,* born 1928–1945, were shaped by economic growth as well as the threat of nuclear war. Post War Cohorts, are more affluent and spend more freely than earlier generations, yet are far more conservative than the generations that follow. These are the current Older People with Active Lifestyles (OPALS) who saved and invested and now offer an attractive market for companies that key into their needs.

- *Baby boomer I cohorts,* born 1946–1954. Members of the Woodstock generation are economic optimists and were profoundly affected by the Kennedy and King assassinations. Feted, chronicled, and catered to since birth, boomers continue to obliterate preconceived marketing notions as they begin turning 50.

- *The baby boomer II or zoomer cohorts.* Born 1955–1965, Boomers II are also known as the Me Generation. Marketers take note. Watergate and downward mobility ensured a less idealistic and optimistic mind set than that of earlier boomers. They spend freely to maintain their way of life.

- *Generation-X cohorts.* Born 1966–1976, this group, also labeled Busters and Slackers, grew up during an era of mixed messages, growing diversity, increasing violence, and uncertainty. Generation X-ers are more likely to have come from broken homes; they entered early adulthood just as the economic boom of the 1980s collapsed and came of age during the AIDS era. They frequently work for modest salaries at jobs for which they are overqualified. X-ers accept ethnic, racial, and sexual diversity to a greater degree than previous generations. Marketers must contend with a generation that is reluctant to be marketed to; but those marketers who can demonstrate quality and added value and who can speak the language of Generation X-ers may be able to convince this market to part with their hard earned money.

Each of these generational cohorts will react in their own way to various cybertraks. But cohorts will not react as a group. Again, we must remember the precepts of particle marketing and overlay many other factors. Each generation is made up of white, African-Americans, Hispanics, Asians, Native Americans, and other races and ethnicities. Educational, regional, and gender differences fragment these generational cohorts further. Do you market to the Mexican community surrounding Chicago as you do to the Mexican community in El Paso? Do you address the gay man in New York's Chelsea area as you would the lesbian in a rural community? Do you sell to an affluent woman in Dallas as you would in San Francisco? What do you think? As we layer in each of these elements we develop particle markets and particles of particles.

In addition, we must consider elements such as household structures. Are you selling to *Dinks* (Dual Income, No Kids) or *Dobies* or *Mobies* (Daddy or Mommy Older, Baby Younger), or perhaps *Buppies* and *Muppies* (Black Urban and Middle-Aged Urban Professionals)? Each demonstrates its own set of consumer behaviors. As Exhibit 25–1 illustrates, the mass market no longer exists. The African-American market, for example, is a particle market which can be broken down into

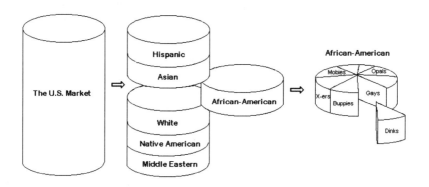

Exhibit 25–1
From Mass . . . to Particles . . . to Particles of Particles

smaller particles such as Dobies, Dinks, Buppies, and Opals. These particles may intersect with other particles such as Generation X-ers or gays and lesbians to create even smaller particles. Today, our challenge is to satisfy the needs of smaller and smaller particles.

So how does all this apply to you? What LinkStrat can you discover or create to link your company's products and services and these major consumer cybertraks? Try this LinkStrat quiz and those in Chapters 26, 27, and 28 to discover your LinkStrats.

HOW TO LINKSTRAT . . .

How well do you know your customers? Datamine your business to complete the charts in Exhibits 25–2 and 25–3.

Can you answer the following questions?

1. Is your product or service something that would be used by someone 55 or older? Would it be if it were repositioned?

2. How can generational marketing improve your company's sales? How can particle marketing help grow sales?

3. Does your advertising and promotion invite African-Americans, Hispanics, or gays and lesbians to purchase your products and services? Or does it exclude them?

	1	2	3
African-Americans			
Chinese American			
Cuban Americans			
Irish Americans			
Italian Americans			
Japanese Americans			
Mexican American			
Native Americans			
Puerto Ricans			
Other Cultures			

Exhibit 25-2
Name 3 Things Different Cultures Would
Like about Your Products/Services

	%
African-Americans	
Chinese American	
Cuban Americans	
Irish Americans	
Italian Americans	
Japanese Americans	
Mexican American	
Native Americans	
Puerto Ricans	
Other Cultures	

Exhibit 25-3
What Percent of Your Products/Services Are
Purchased by the Following Cultures?

26

Cybertrak—
Electronic Commerce

Fact or Fiction?

*The Information Highway will transform our culture as
dramatically as Gutenburg's press did the Middle Ages.*

Bill Gates, CEO, Microsoft,
author of *The Road Ahead*

Get ready to boot up your television. It's a battle for
the eyeballs and the fingertips of the world. Is it
fact or is it fiction? Has the fight for real estate
space truly become a fight for cyberspace? Do you
believe that in the future we will build businesses
without bricks and mortar? Is electronic commerce
a bona fide cybertrak or just a media blip? Do you
believe, like many, that it's no longer a fight for a
marketplace but for *marketspace*—that territory in
cyberspace where commercial interests compete?

Welcome to the "battle for the eyeballs" where
electronic media, retailers, manufacturers, service
firms, and many others vie for the attention of the
consumer/customer. Here the small entrepreneur
and the conglomerate have an opportunity to send

223

their message and market their products and services in a way that has never been done before. You say you don't buy it?

Well, this country has a history of dismissing new ways of doing business. Were you one of those who said, "Outlet stores and warehouse clubs will never happen. Vendors don't dare sell directly to consumers"? Or "Wal-Mart? That's strictly for the boonies." If you want to join the lack-of-fore-sight club, it's not too late. Just say, "Electronic commerce will never happen. That's for computer nerds and people with nothing to do but watch television all day."

Electronic commerce is happening now. Measuring dollar volume, however, is virtually impossible. We do know that cable TV home shopping accounts for about $4 billion in sales. But do you also include transactions between importers and exporters who are connecting via Internet bulletin boards? Or the millions of daily transactions over ATM machines? Or the sales generated by CD-ROM marketing presentations? And with over 80,000 web sites on the World Wide Web—many commercial—who's toting up that dollar volume?

Conservative estimates say that between 12 to 15 million Americans are now on-line either through services such as America Online or connected directly to the Internet. An estimated 30 million are connected world wide. As electronic banking becomes more accepted with Microsoft and Intuit competing to connect banks with customers, more consumers and businesses will find reason to get wired. Be warned. You ignore electronic commerce at your own peril.

The scope of this new mode of commerce is extremely broad, affecting the marketing plans of just about any company that has a product or service it wants to sell. With technology as the enabler, electronic commerce is truly boundaryless with global implications.

What then is electronic commerce? It is the application of new electronic technology to the marketplace in a number of evolving forms. It is conducting business and shopping via such on-line services as America Online or via the Internet; it's CD-ROMs and digital interactive television; it's kiosks, infomercials, and cable home shopping channels.

While all applications of the new electronic technology are *not* for all companies, at least one application should affect your company soon. Addressing the strategic value of these applications and finding LinkStrats that connect your business are imperative. One important reason: traditional marketing channels in the United States have matured. The days when a retailer, for example, could expand (at enormous cost) by riding the wave of mall development are over. Micropockets of untapped consumers still exist in many areas, but reaching them through traditional retailing is no longer economical.

But existing opportunities can be addressed through electronic commerce. As the consumer (and business customer) becomes accustomed to shopping in these new and nontraditional ways, businesses will be able to capture that consumer or customer in whichever market he is shopping. Electronic commerce will also allow companies to get inside more micropockets of business and to take advantage of generational shifts.

■ Preparing for Generational Shifts

If your business is limited to the 60- to 75-year-old+ market, chances are, electronic commerce isn't playing a big part in your business today. The 60 to 75+ generation is *generally* not computer savvy and has little interest in learning to use computers. However, moving down the generational chain toward graying baby boomers, we find increased technical savvy. As they grow older, baby boomers will be comfortable shopping on-line, via digital television, and all the other electronic ways of doing business.

Generation X-ers and the millennium generation are as comfortable with the new technology as older generations are with television. Going on-line, digital, interactive, and paging through a CD-ROM catalog will be second nature for these younger people whether they are shopping as consumers or as business customers. So, if you're not yet on the information superhighway, it's time to become technologically aware or be left at the side of the road with a dwindling pool of customers.

The rise of digital shopping will create new retailing and manufacturing giants and reconfigure business processes. Electronic commerce offers those who master its technological and marketing requirements, the potential for both global reach and targeted micromarketing. It will provide new customers and new ways to reach old customers without the expense of additional personnel or retail space. Along the way, it will profoundly affect real estate values, employment opportunities, trafficking, and retail financing.

Some major businesses, such as Levi Strauss & Co., Nike, Reebok, Ben and Jerry's, Godiva, Ragu, PC Flowers, Spiegel's, Eddie Bauer, and Land's End, have already recognized the potential and are adopting electronic home shopping to reach existing customers in new ways and to introduce themselves to new customers.

For the manufacturer or brand name owner, electronic commerce opens up new ways to sell directly to the consumer. Businesses can expand their operations without the cost of bricks and mortar and extend their hours without hiring additional personnel. They can also speed up the business cycle by getting immediate consumer response to new products and services. They reduce the costs of shipping to individual stores, bringing products through receiving, merchandising them on the floor, educating salespeople, and advertising in local media. Instead, the product is put before the public on television or a computer, then shipped directly to the consumer in response to sales.

Vendors who go directly to the public reduce the expense of marketing their products and services through retailers. That means lower prices for the consumer and greater profits for the manufacturer or service provider. Electronic home shopping also offers businesses opportunities to test in local markets before going national.

Business to business marketers are servicing customers and finding new markets in cyberspace. Every day, thousands of Federal Express customers track packages through the company's Web site. UPS began offering a similar service in 1995. With easy access to computers, on-line corporate purchasing and shopping via CD-ROM catalogs will save purchasers time and money and make access to new customers cheaper and easier for business vendors.

The growth of electronic commerce is developing on six major fronts (see Exhibit 26–1).

- *TV home shopping* is the largest and most established participant in the electronic shopping arena with current sales of approximately $4 billion. Despite recent slowdowns, triple digit growth is expected for the early years of the 21st century as manufacturers, brand name owners, traditional retailers, and new virtual retailers all discover the potential of e-shopping. The Home Shopping Network and QVC have laid the groundwork for newer shopping networks, such as VIA-TV, which will take advantage of fiber optics technology that will provide consumers access to a 500-channel system.

- *Infomercials* are the grand daddy of electronic commerce. Remember those late night commercials from the 1950s? "It chops; it slices; it grates"? Infomercials have grown up. The National Infomercial Marketing Association (NIMA) estimates the infomercial industry sells $1 billion in goods and services annually. The format is ideal for selling such products as computers

Types of E-Commerce	Advantages	Weaknesses	Market Appeal
Kiosks	. Can be placed where needed . Can be interactive . Can be adapted to many needs . High consumer comfort level	. Can't reach the consumer at home . Can be vandalized	. General appeal, thanks to ATM's
On-Line (Web sites and Internet	. Interactive . Reaches consumers at home . Can reach businesses in the office . Economical . Boundary-less	. Can only reach computer owners	. Younger consumers, Boomers down
Intranet	. Communicates within a business to multisite locations. . Economical . Interactive		. Staff within company
TV Home Shopping	. Potential to reach most homes . User friendly	. Considered down market . Consumer has no control	. Older customers
Interactive TV	. Puts the customer in charge . Speeds up the buying process	. We're still waiting	. Remains to be seen
CD-ROMs	. It's multi-media. . Delivers professional sales message . Young people think it's cool . Economical	. Must have computer with CD-ROM	. Business-to-business marketers. . Catalog shoppers . Boomers and younger
Infomercials	. Can deliver detailed sales message . Format allows for creativity	. Must overcome tacky image.	. General market . Insomniacs

Exhibit 26–1
Electronic Commerce

or galleries of furniture that require detailed explanation of workmanship, fabrics, and finishes. Watch for more brand name manufacturers and retailers to join Apple, Ford, and Mattel in bringing respectability to the medium.

- *Digital kiosks.* The 21st century version of the vending machine, digital kiosks are virtual sales and service personnel. Currently ATMs are the most widespread and successful use of kiosk technology. They've become an integral part of our lifestyles. In-store and stand-alone kiosks will be used increasingly to provide consumer information and perform sales transactions. Portable digital kiosks can place brands in airports, supermarkets, or football stadiums.

- *On-line computing.* Shopping on the Internet and through other computer direct sources is a major growth area. More than 30 million people surf the Internet globally, according to *BusinessWeek.* In the United States, 12 to 15 million consumers subscribe to on-line services such as America Online. With the introduction of Microsoft's Windows 95 and its companion Microsoft Network software, millions of additional computer owners are connecting to the Internet.

- *CD-ROMs.* Multimedia CD-ROMs not only pack a tremendous amount of information, but can also offer sound, graphics, and full motion video—all on one lightweight CD. That makes them an ideal medium for catalogers such as J.C. Penney. It also makes them an attractive tool for businesses that want to be sure all their customers receive top-flight marketing presentations. Sales representatives, from consumer product companies to industrial equipment manufacturers, are taking their laptops and CD-ROMs wherever their customers are.

- *Interactive TV.* Still in its infancy, Interactive TV will eventually realize the full potential of electronic commerce. Interactive TV allows the consumer to select merchandise, spending as much time as he wants comparing various styles and brands. Then the consumer can automatically purchase the product by punching in numbers on the TV remote. Digital interactive TV may take the lead in electronic commerce sales as it becomes available throughout the country.

As merchandise on demand, comparison shopping, more brand names, and quality products become available to electronic commerce customers, sales will grow exponentially. Manufacturers, brand name owners, distributors, and retailers all have opportunities to maximize their profit potential if they think of electronic home shopping as a tool at their display rather than competition. Think of e-shopping as an additional way to reach new consumers and more consumers more frequently.

As an added bonus, electronic commerce marketers, can build essential data bases including frequency patterns, consumer names, and product interests for datamining. Electronic commerce will allow companies to build a business that is in better touch with its customers and far more responsive to their needs.

Start looking for the LinkStrats that connect your business to electronic commerce and the customers it offers. First consider the various strategic links of your business and gain a firm understanding of the different technological applications that are available. Then you will begin to understand how you can use electronic commerce strategically.

HOW TO LINKSTRAT . . .

To help find your electronic commerce LinkStrats complete the charts in Exhibits 26–2 and 26–3. In the first column of Exhibit 26–2, list those products or services which you feel could be successfully marketed via electronic commerce. In the second column, fill in the form of electronic commerce that would offer the best channel for that product. Then, in the third column, indicate why you would choose that type of electronic commerce.

In Exhibit 26–3 decide what percentage of your customers might be reached by the six types of electronic commerce today. What percentage might be reached via those channels in five years. Finally, indicate how the changes over that five year period might change your product or service.

Now answer the following questions:

1. If some of your customers are surfing the net, where will you find them? America Online? At which outposts on the Web?

2. Is your sales force presenting customers with the message marketing wants to convey? Can CD-ROM technology help you tell your story in a more effective and exciting way?

3. What are the best-selling categories of products on home shopping TV programs? Do any of your products belong there?

4. Are the cost of rent and the availability of trained sales personnel keeping your business from realizing its potential? Can electronic commerce alleviate this problem?

5. Are you a business-to-business marketer? If so, how might you design business-to-business opportunities within a Web site for your company?

Product/Service	Type of E-Commerce	Why?

Exhibit 26–2
Which of Your Products/Services Could Be Marketed via Electronic Commerce?

Type of Electronic Commerce	Est. Percentage Today	Est. Percentage In 5 Years	How Does This Change Your Product/Service?
Kiosks			
On-Line (Web sites, Internet)			
Intranet			
TV Home Shopping			
Interactive TV			
CD-Roms			
Infomercials			

Exhibit 26–3
Where Can You Find Your Customers?

27

Cybertrak

The Virtual Office

You got to be careful if you don't know where you're going, because you might not get there.

Yogi Berra, American baseball player

During the better part of the 20th century, American business was obsessed with bricks and mortar. A company that could emblazon its name on a building in Los Angeles, Chicago, or New York was to be reckoned with. Better yet, hire I.M. Pei or Philip Johnson to create a bold architectural statement consistent with the company's image.

As we move into the 21st century, American business is fast losing its edifice complex. Today bricks and mortar may just be outdated real estate. Welcome to the world of the virtual office—another important cybertrak—where, thanks to laptops and teleconferencing, your office address may be just an internet address.

While no one is predicting the total demise of the traditional office, its role will be downplayed in the century ahead. The "office," whether it was company headquarters, a regional sales office, or a service facility, once provided essential functions. It supplied access to people—bosses, coworkers, and secretaries—as well as to records, information, and equipment. And how would anyone get his little pink message slips without a receptionist? The laptop computer, with its e-mail, fax, copier, and document storage capabilities has effectively replaced many of those functions freeing employees be where the action is—with the customer.

In fact, the computer and forms of interactivity and telecommunications allow employees to work just about anywhere—hotels, rented work spaces, airplanes, and home. As the costs of teleconferencing and televideoing come down, watch this trend accelerate.

That's just one aspect of the changing world of business. Old management structures and values are crumbling along with bricks and mortar. The career path for the ambitious young man or woman was once clear. Start at the bottom and work your way up—from the mail room to the executive suite. But the shape of business is changing.

The 20th-century office resembled a pyramid (Exhibit 27–1) that placed platoons of typists, clerks, and assistants at the bottom. Next layer up were the assistant managers and senior secretaries, then middle managers. Above them were the senior managers, then the vice presidents. As you rose to the top, the ranks grew thinner until, twinkling at the apex like a star on a Christmas tree, was the CEO.

Directives were sent from the top down, while employees reported from the bottom up. Eager junior managers competed with one another aiming to take another step up the ladder. Each promotion meant a more impressive title and command over a greater number of people. Managers guarded their territories fiercely. The structure provided little incentive to cooperate or work cross-departmentally.

The virtual office looks more like Exhibit 27–2. New technology has eliminated many lower level jobs, while

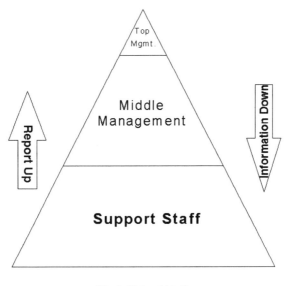

Exhibit 27–1
20th Century Office

downsizing and reengineering has thinned the ranks of junior and middle management. Even the way information flows has changed. Today information flows laterally as well as vertically. Indeed, with e-mail the most likely flow is from computer to computer. Instantly.

A major change is reduced management hierarchy. With no corporate ladder to climb, employees can turn their attention to more productive activities such as creating and building business. Today that means working cross-departmentally. Using a project approach to business development, self-managing employees form teams drawing key members from various areas of the company to contribute their skills to the project. As projects are completed, the team disbands and employees move on to other teams and other projects. The rewards are not titles and corner offices, but the opportunity to build skills and a portfolio of experience (Exhibit 27–3).

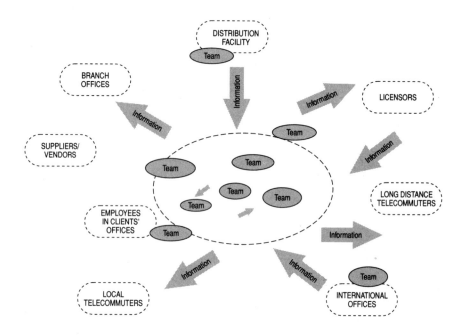

Exhibit 27–2
The Virtual Office

Factors	20th Century O & M	21st Century O & M
Company structure	Rigid	In flux
Management shape	Pyramid	Lateral oval
Career movement	Vertical	Lateral
Rewards	Perks and titles	Skill building
Focus	Boss-oriented	Customer-oriented
Valued behavior	Following orders	Taking initiative
Work modes	Flying solo	Teaming
Peer attitudes	Competitive	Cooperative

Exhibit 27–3
Are You on the 21st Century Office
and Management Cybertrak?

Some of the employees who comprise those teams may not be "company people" but temporary or freelance workers. Temps were once strictly secretaries, clerks, and blue-collar workers who were called in to substitute for vacationing staff or help out during the busy season. Today they are more likely to fill executive or professional posts. Doctors, lawyers, engineers, and others are now making careers from outsourcing assignments.

We've already come a long way from 20th-century office and management, which resembled the military complete with strict rules, rewards for obedience, and a well-defined chain of command. The troops, who often signed on for life, stood guard at the fort or corporate headquarters. 21st century office and management is the apotheoses. The fort has no walls and the chain of command changes minute by minute. Innovation is valued over obedience, and those who wait to be told what to do will end up doing little. It's a "Brave New World." Are you ready for it? Try this test.

	Need to Be There	Don't Need to Be There
Important	Quadrant I	Quadrant II
Not Important	Quadrant III	Quadrant IV

Exhibit 27–4
Are You Ready for the Virtual Office?

1. Draw four quadrants as shown in Exhibit 27–4.

2. On a separate sheet of paper list *all* activities that take up your time, such as planning, budgeting, power breakfasts, and reading business journals.

3. Now place each item on your list in the appropriate quadrant. For example, important activities that require your presence at the office go in Quadrant I. Unimportant activities that don't require your presence in the office go in Quadrant IV.

4. Okay, look at Quadrants I and II. How many activities do you have in each? Does that tell how ready you are for the virtual office?

HOW TO LINKSTRAT . . .

Ask yourself the following questions. They may help you build LinkStrats to take your company closer to the virtual office.

1. Do I need to be in my office now as much as I did before? What about my team members? Would our time be better spent elsewhere?

2. Could I share my office or do I need an office at all?

3. Can I have a follow-me phone number wherever I go?

4. What information do my team members and I need that keeps us office-bound? Is there a system that could make that information portable?

5. Should I have a laptop? Or, what more can my laptop do for me?

28

Cybertrak— Global Marketing

You've Got the Whole World in Your Hands

A man's feet must be planted in his country, but his eyes should survey the world.

George Santayana, philosopher

Facts:

- 95 percent of the world's population lies outside the United States.
- By the year 2000, 90 percent of the top 100 retailers will be global. Seven out of ten are today.
- The U.S. market has matured and offers fewer growth opportunities for marketers.

Whether your company manufactures business forms, provides a service to businesses, or retails fashion apparel, if you set your sights no farther than the geographic boundaries of the United

States, you limit your prospects. With no population explosion on the horizon nor prospects for an economic boom, there are no longer any free rides to sales success within U.S. borders.

Baby boomers fueled a consumer spending boom unlike any in U.S. history. But as those boomers move into middle age, they are adopting more conservative spending habits. Higher living expenses, tight monetary policy, and stricter regulations of financial institutions coupled with a major shift in consumer values has led to a cooling of consumer spending. America is over-retailed and over-stored. During the past decade, many retailers have died off or been absorbed into other operations. That trend continues as we approach the 21st century.

As the United States moved into market maturity, the rest of the world has grown more consumer-oriented. Europe, Japan, and the newly industrialized countries of Asia and Latin America have experienced a dramatic upswing in living standards. Governments are encouraging their countries to become more consumer-oriented. Japan, for example, is urging employers to offer workers more leisure time with the aim of stimulating sales and decreasing the extremely high rate of savings.

When global consumers go looking for new products to buy, chances are they will ask for Western products—particularly American brands. Satellite television has spurred the demand for westernized goods. As it moves into the many regions of the world, brands are becoming globally accepted. Coca-Cola, the most global of all brands, has led the way for other beverage and food marketers such as Campbell's, McDonald's, Pizza Hut, Pepsi Cola, and Burger King. Even American service brands such as UPS and Fedex carry cachet abroad.

Traditionally, Europeans have been more at ease with international trade than Americans. They have a history of selling across national boundaries and are accustomed to communicating in foreign languages. Luxury producers such as Louis Vuitton and Hermes have long felt at home in the United States. Middle market-oriented retailers such as IKEA and Benetton have established themselves in the United States, while companies such as Carrefour and Gallerie Lafayette have tried and failed.

Americans, conversely, are frequently intimidated by language barriers. Unaccustomed to dealing with tariffs, import duties, and the intricacies of marketing into foreign cultures, they fall back on the belief that the United States, as the largest and most powerful economic force in the world, is an inexhaustible market. Even so, some aggressive Americans are getting a big jump on global marketing. In the retail arena, Staples, the office products superstore, is moving into Germany, Israel, and the United Kingdom. The Price Club is operating in Mexico, and J.C. Penney and Dillards are looking to do the same. Toys R Us has successfully taken its formula global. Wal-Mart is entering China, Hong Kong, Latin America, Mexico, Canada, and Europe and by the end of the century will be one of the top global players. Global sales account for 56 percent of Motorola's volume. Manufacturers as varied as Levi Strauss & Co. and Estee Lauder have gone international, and Avon already seems to be everywhere. Smaller companies with more modest brand names are also carving out global markets. Besides Apple and IBM, many computer manufacturers, such as Gateway 2000, are enjoying early success.

Though these companies may have "the whole world in their hands," they are aware that global development will travel from mature economies, such as those of Western Europe, to frontier economies, including Latin America, Southeast Asia, Southeastern Europe and China.

The global picture is changing rapidly. By the year 2000, Western Europe will be well on the way to adopting a single currency. Eastern Europe is ready for a new retail industry and is becoming an increasingly consumer-oriented region.

All of Europe is ready for retail formats such as discounting, category killers, niche retailing, warehouse clubs, etc. Latin America is ripe for growth, but the Asian economy will grow fastest. Throughout Asia, consumers are experiencing a rapidly rising standard of living.

Many business executives still feel that "going global" is limited to giants such as Coca-Cola and General Motors. Certainly a globally-oriented company must have the resources to explore the cultural, business, and legal differences among countries. But developing that understanding is not beyond the capacity of the midsized and even smaller firm.

International marketers must be sensitive to the ways of other cultures, just as they are sensitive to the ways of various ethnic groups right at home. Despite differences, there are important, essential similarities among consumers around the world. Global communications has united the world. Television instantly transmits news, sports, and entertainment events via satellite, building a commonality of experience. Popular music and movies create familiarity and admiration for our way of life. American movie and rock stars are better known than presidents. Computers, fax machines, and telephones create a web of communications that link individuals and business. This communications and media revolution has created a market of global consumers, who can be segmented into five major markets.

- *The worldly wealthy.* The rich are the original global consumers. With money to travel extensively, for centuries they have traveled from Paris, to London, to Milan—wherever the best was sold. Now purveyors of elite wares—from fashions to food products—are going global, opening outposts around the world. Wealthy Japanese traveling in New York City, Beverly Hills, or Chicago purchase Hermes scarves and Louis Vuitton bags. Saudi princes buy Land Rovers and

Tiffany silver. The retailer or producer of an elite product with brand equity knows no trade boundaries.

- *Comfortably older.* Like OPALS in the United States, the comfortably older consumer is a force throughout the developed world where populations are aging. As children finish school and leave home, these empty nesters have increased discretionary income and the time to enjoy it. Like their counterparts in the United States, they place a high premium on quality, but are also value-oriented. Since today's older consumers are likely to be healthier and lead a more active lifestyle than the older customers of 20 years ago, they are a particularly attractive market for products and services related to leisure activities, education, and travel.

- *Pampered kids.* In developed countries around the world, consumers lavish money on products for their children—clothing, toys, video games, consumer electronics, compact discs, and sporting goods. The same products and brand names are popular worldwide. Amazingly, teens in Iran or Nepal can be more tuned to the youth culture than adults right here in the United States. Build your brand with the youth of the world and you build brand loyalty that can last a lifetime.

- *The emerging middle class.* In countries as diverse as Argentina, Korea, India, and Turkey, a formidable middle class is emerging. They are demanding the same goods and services American and European consumers enjoy. Their buying patterns even reflect those of Americans. They are willing to pay a premium for high quality, brand name items, while demanding value pricing on basics and necessities. They are an ideal market for retailing formats such as discounting, category killers and niche marketers. The emerging middle class of developing countries offers global marketers their greatest opportunities.

- *Women on the job.* Women have become a major force in the workplace in most countries, creating a particular strong market for convenience products. Marketers of home appliances, convenience foods, time-saving services, and work-appropriate apparel have an enormous international market to tap.

As challenging as global marketing may be, it is often easier than launching a new product in the United States. The company has already tested its marketing plan domestically. It has conducted a dress rehearsal at home selling to the domestic version of the comfortably older, the pampered kids or woman in the workplace.

Where do you begin? First, know that global marketing is not limited to big companies, world famous brand names, consumer product manufacturers, or renowned retailers. There is room for many different types of companies on the global stage. Licensing and joint venture formats are just two ways that the smaller company can enter the competition. And the technological enabler of marketing on the Internet has created a more level playing field for small and midsize companies. Second, understand that the opportunities to establish a company as a global entity exists now. The window of opportunity will slam shut. Why?

■ GATT, NAFTA . . . And They're Off and Running

The passage of NAFTA and the recent GATT rounds signal the beginning of a new era in open trade. Opportunities in Canada, Mexico, and other nations are more favorable than ever before. Companies that have been waiting for their opportunity must move now or be edged out. And technology is making the clock tick even faster. Companies that begin going global will be challenged, and only the best managed, most adaptable, most innovative companies will succeed. Today we do have the whole world in our hands—but those will be busy hands. Companies will be doing a juggling act between outbound needs—going global and exporting to world markets—and inbound needs—sourcing world markets.

Whatever their product or service, all companies should seriously consider:

- Finding partners to reduce risk.
- Developing strategic integrity. All activities must be ethical and professional.
- Enlisting counsel in international law and taxes.
- Delegating execution. Find an experienced international marketer to head your globalization efforts.
- Seeking opportunities to go native. You must work with and build partnerships with the natives of the soil.
- Being diligent and patient. In other cultures, business is developed over years and traders develop "good life partners." Your foreign partners and customers want to know you are serious and plan to stay.
- Being aware of the foreign culture and the many, varied tastes of people.

So if your vision and mission are global and you believe an international business can be integrated into your company, begin by reiterating the LINKS process. To uncover the opportunities that lie outside United States boundaries, start by asking yourself, and your team, "What if?" What if we were to market service Y in the Far East? What if we were to license product X in Great Britain? Find the primary and secondary assumptions associated with your core odea. Ask what your competition is doing or may do in those areas. Then decide what opportunities and lie ahead.

```
. Organization
. Expertise
. Financials
. Brand Equity
. Markets
. Products and Services
. Sourcing Needs
. Partnering
. Joint Ventures
. Tax Treaties and Tariff Issues
. Licensing
```

Exhibit 28–1
Going Global: Critical Issues

Once you have found your opportunities, you will begin the critical tasks involved in implementation (Exhibit 28–1). The process requires time, investment, and commitment. Is it worth it? Look at the annual reports of companies like Motorola, Campbell's, Coca-Cola, or many smaller companies that are growing globally. What's in it for you? The answer to that is new markets, new consumers, and more dollars, pesos, or rubles.

Do you and your team thoroughly understand...	Yes	No
The cultures of the host countries?		
The governments?		
Tax structures?		
Joint ventures?		
Licensing?		
Are you committed for the long term?		
Have you made "good life" partners abroad?		

Exhibit 28–2
Is Your Company Ready for Global Marketing?

HOW TO LINKSTRAT . . .

Now take the first step to finding the LinkStrats that will build bridges between your company and the potential of global marketing. Complete the chart in Exhibit 28–2 and then ask yourself the following questions:

1. Which of our products or services can we envision being used in France, Brazil, India?
2. Which international consumer group best suits our products and services? For example, The comfortably older? The working woman?
3. Are we willing to commit long term (five years) to globalization?
4. How will our brand adapt to various foreign markets?
5. In what ways could we adapt our products or services to fit the needs of foreign markets?

29

Out of the Box

This part of a book is usually referred to as the epilogue, summary, or conclusion. It's the place where the author ties the concepts together in a neat package and sends the reader off with a few homilies and some well chosen words of encouragement.

Strategic marketing and the LINKS process, however, don't present a neat package. Instead they offer constant, continuous change. Everything—your company and its departments or divisions, your people, your industry, your world—is in constant flux. Each piece keeps changing, reacting and interacting with every other piece. Nothing is ever done, fixed, finished, or over. Sure, you can still take a week off to go kayaking. But don't think anything stops while you're gone. It doesn't. Ever. No matter how well you know your business, you will never have it figured out, because there will always be something new to figure in. That's just the way business is in the real time 21st century.

I'd love to tell you that having read this book, you are now completely armed, strategically and tactically, to do battle in the increasingly competitive business world. But, how well armed you are depends upon you, your team, and your collective willingness to continually pursue success and put to work the tools that have been presented here.

The processes, strategies, and tactics that we have discussed are ongoing too, which makes complete sense. If your company is changing every day, you can't expect the strategic assessment you do this year to be the only strategic assessment you will ever need to do. Strategic assessment and planning is an ongoing process. As soon as you have worked your way through the LINKS process, each of the Strategic Links, and the tactical phases of strategy implementation, you're ready to go back and start over.

Now, a few words of encouragement. The first time through is the most difficult. It is totally new territory for many of you. It's often a completely new way of thinking. But if you KISS it, involve your key people, and allow time for the process to work, you will see progress. As you repeat the process in future years, you will gain a deeper and richer understanding of your company, your customers, and your capabilities. You

Exhibit 29–1
Out of the Box

will find that planning, controls, and measurements for success will make life easier and more predictable.

You will also discover that the more open atmosphere and flow of communication which the New Consumerism and the New Marketing demand create a very positive and welcome change in your Culture Factor. You will also see that operating in Real Time quickly becomes addictive. You will never want to go back to the "any day now" way of doing business. Of course, you couldn't if you wanted to. Right now, change is happening faster than at any point in history. We either become a part of that change or are left behind.

The 21st century is nearly upon us. Like the man in Exhibit 29-1, will you be ready for it?

 **APPENDIX**

The "Get Ready, Get Set, Go" Checklist

Let's do a quick review to be sure you have taken all the important steps along the way to finding your future. To make sure you and your team are ready to realize your strategic marketing plan, review this brief checklist.

1. Have you formed your strategic assessment team?
   ❑ Yes   ❑ No

2. Have you and the team gone through the LINKS process at least once?
   ❑ Yes   ❑ No

3. Did you arrive at your Opportunities?
   ❑ Yes   ❑ No

4. Have you created your Vision Statement?
   ❑ Yes   ❑ No

5. Did you write your Mission Statement and formulate your objectives?
   ❑ Yes   ❑ No

6. Have you analyzed your Company Culture and how you can mold it to fit your Mission?
   ❑ Yes   ❑ No

7. Are your marketing and sales departments keyed into the New Consumerism?
   ❑ Yes   ❑ No

8. If you are branded, do you have a plan for growing your brand's equity?
   ❏ Yes   ❏ No

9. Do you know how consumer trends or trends among your customers will affect your company's future?
   ❏ Yes   ❏ No

10. Are you learning about electronic commerce, the Internet, and the virtual office and how they will affect your business?
   ❏ Yes   ❏ No

If you have said no to even one of these questions, go back and work through the appropriate chapter. In the next two chapters, we provide some tools to ease the way—hot buzzwords and technoterms and worthwhile web addresses.

Today's Technoterms, Buzzwords, and Neologisms . . . and How to Use Them

With the proliferation of new ideas and advancements in technology, business, and marketing, the old pegs don't do the job anymore. Every time we open a newspaper, turn on the television, or log-on to the Internet, we find new terminology coined to describe some recently-discovered demographic segment or new turn on the Information Superhighway. How up-to-date is your vocabulary? Take this 3 minute test and find out. Just choose the answer that you feel is the best definition for the following words.

1. *Infonaut*
   - ❏ A. A public relations person at NASA.
   - ❏ B. A corporation's chief information officer.
   - ❏ C. A member of the Yankees' new farm team.
2. *Doby*
   - ❏ A. The lead character on a 1950s sitcom.
   - ❏ B. Demographics acronym for family unit with baby and older father.
   - ❏ C. A new computer operating system.
3. *PGP (Pretty Good Privacy)*
   - ❏ A. New rules protecting consumers against unscrupulous telemarketers.

    ❑ B. The most popular cryptosystem on the Internet.

    ❑ C. Bill Gates' favorite grunge rock group.

4. *Chunking*

    ❑ A. Manufacturer and marketer of Chinese foods.

    ❑ B. Management technique for dealing with segments of business.

    ❑ C. A method of transferring information over a network.

5. *Disintermediation*

    ❑ A. The failure of labor and management to come to an agreement.

    ❑ B. Eliminating the middleman.

    ❑ C. A $5 word for sexual harassment.

For the correct answers, read "Technoterms for the Next Millennium" on pages 259–261.

Digital Communications, Computerese

Access	The means to gain entry to a computer system.
Access Control	Method for limiting access to a computer system.
Authorized User	Individual allowed access to an organization's computer network.
Authenticated User	An authorized user whose identity has been confirmed.
Bulletin Board	Sites on the Internet to post messages or share ideas/
Client/Server Computing	Networks which use a powerful "server" computer to feed programs and data to smaller computers.
Cyberpolice	Those who want to censor sexually explicit or violent on-line sites.
Cyberspace	The universe of networked computers.
Digital Homeless	Executives who have tuned in to Cyberspace.
Dual-Homed Gateway	Gateway that hides an organization's internal network from the Internet.
EDI	Electronic Data Interchange
E-mail	Electronic Mail. Message can be sent globally or within the boundaries of a company from one computer to another.
Fibersphere	Refers to massive capacity of fiber optics and the universe of fiber optics communications.
Firewall	A device that protects a computer system and the organization's data from unauthorized users on other computer networks.
Flaming	Cyberspace version of a dressing-down usually for an infraction of the Internet code of good behavior.
Gateway	A computer that handles messages and data that moves from one network to another.
Groupware	Business computing for the 90s. A combination of software and hardware that allows groups to see and work on the same file at the time.
Half-duplex	Internet phone conversation allowing only one person to talk at a time.
Internet	The global matrix of connecting computers
Intranet	An organization's private internal network.
Killer Apps	Large, highly effective computer applications.
Kobrigram	A legal threat in response to an on-line statement. Named for Helena Kobrin, a Church of Scientology lawyer who has been threatening lawsuits against on-liners whose actions have displeased the church.
LAN	Local Area Network
Mission-Critical Computing	If it goes, the company goes. Computing essential to the company's ability to function.
Multimedia Publishing	Publishing using computer sound, graphics, text and full motion video.
PGP	Pretty Good Privacy. The most popular Internet cryptosystem.
Screamers	Super fast computers.
Site	Any spot on-line that can be tapped for information.
Snail Mail	Computerese for the U.S. Postal Service.
Software Mainframe	See Virtual Mainframe.
Surfing the Net	Sampling the spectrum of Internet offerings.
Telecosm	Telephone communications universe.
Telephony	Computer-related communications including faxes, voice messages, data communications, and digital audio.
Virtual Mainframe	PC's which use network software that emulates a mainframe.
The Web	User-friendly nickname for the World Wide Web
Web Words	The lexicon of Cyberspace
World Wide Web	The vast network of sites or home pages on the Internet. Educators, businesses, publishers, individuals, and others combine information, graphics, full motion video, sound, and links that move Internet surfers from site to site.

(Continued)

Technoterms for the Next Millennium

259

Marketing Terms and Miscellany

Begathon	Telethons and other media fund-raisers that use heart-tugging tactics.
Benchmarking	Assessing and measuring a company's results by comparing them to industry standards.
BPR	Business Process Reengineering
Chunking	Management technique in which segments of business are dealt with in chunks or large pieces.
Coaching	A human resources, training and development term referring to an informal approach to improving employee skills in which a supervisor, acting like a sports coach, advises employees in attaining work goals.
Cybertraks	Major trends leading us into the 21st Century.
Datamine	To dig out all the nuggets of information in a consumer/customer database to better understand and satisfy the consumers' or customers' needs and wants.
Demass	To go from mass market to particle marketing.
Disintermediation	Getting rid of the middleman.
Downsizing	An attempt to increase profits by eliminating unprofitable divisions, stores, products, and accounts.
ECR	Efficient Consumer Response. The result of reengineering distribution channel communications to provide optimum flow of information.
EVC	Electronic Value Chain (The value chain as influenced by electronic commerce.)
Evolution, not revolution	Relates to the need for marketing changes to be rooted in existing business and assets.
Pharming	Pharmaceutical farming--the genetic engineering of crops to protect them and consumers whose eat them from disease.
Generational Marketing	Marketing methodology which groups consumers as "cohorts" based on their meaningful coming-of-age experiences.
Glocal	Global products, local marketing and sales.
Goal Tracking	Any system which tracks the achievement of goals.
Gray Matter	Older, more experienced employees hired by young entrepreneurs to make a company appear more established.
Homing	Trend toward homes becoming self-sufficient units as home-based business grow and consumers spend more personal time in the home.
JIT	Just in Time systems aim to keep a flow of products moving toward market in the quantities needed at the time needed. Used in grocery industry.
LinkStrats	The links that exist or are created to connect a company and its products or services to a major Cybertrak.
Marketspace	A product or service's commercial niche on the Internet.
QR	Quick Response. The apparel industry answer to JIT. QR aims to shorten cycle that brings products to market. Relies heavily on EDI.
Reengineering	Examining and rethinking every facet of a business to build a more effective and efficient organization.
Selling Is Communicating	A phrase that underscores importance of continuous two-way communications between vendor and buyer in the selling relationship.
Teaming	A management approach in which small groups or teams are formed to to accomplish specific tasks.
To that point	Newspeak for "regarding your concern or issue."
TQM	Total Quality Management
Web Space	A company's place in Cyberspace
YODA	Young Opinionated Directionless Artiste. All-talk-and-no-action types who hold forth in coffee houses and other forums for the disaffected.

Demographic, Consumer Terms

Buppies	Black Urban Professionals
Cohorts	Related to Generational Marketing, Cohorts are those who have shared and been shaped by common experiences such as World War II or the Depression.
Dinks	Dual Income, No Kids couples
Dobies	Daddy Older, Baby Younger
Echo Generation	The children of the Baby Boomers
Generation X-ers	Today's young adults, ages 19 to 29. Also called Slackers.
Millennium Generation	The generation coming of age with the new millennium.
Mobies	Mommy Older, Baby Younger
Muppies	Middle-aged Urban Professionals
Opals	Older People with Active Lifestyles
Yuppies	Young Urban Professionals

Directory: Absolutely Essential Addresses on the Internet

So you're on-line. You've entered the Internet and you're eager to see what the World Wide Web is all about. Now what? Here are a few addresses that will put you on the fast track. A word of warning, however. Web pages are constantly changing and moving. That means new addresses and new content. Don't worry, you'll be an expert in no time after trying the addresses given on pages 264–266.

Home Page	Address	Content
Cultural & Culinary		
BookWeb	http://www.ambook.org/bookweb/	An on-line version of *The New York Review of Books*
Electronic Gourmet Guide (eGG)	http://www/2way.com/food/egg/index.html	Everything from food history to new recipes in this e-zine for gourmets.
Epicurious	http://www.epicurious.com/epicurious/home.html	Conde Nast's (Gourmet, Bon Appetit) Cyberzine for food lovers.
French Wines and Foods	http://www.frenchwinesfood.com/index.html	Need help finding the perfect wine to go with Coquille St. Jacques?
The Louvre	http://www.paris.org/Musees/Louvre	Tour the Louvre and find the museum on a Metro map.
Movielink	http://www.777film.com/	What's playing where? Is it worth $7.50, plus hot buttered corn?
The Music of Windham Hill	http://www.windham.com/our.music/	Music and video samples from Windham Hill CD's: rock, blues, and contemporary instrumentals, plus sheet music and songbooks.
the place	gertrude.art.uiuc.edu/ludgate/the/place.html	Displays art created specifically for the Web.
Smithsonian Institute	http://www.si.edu/	Visit the Smithsonian or link into other museums.
The Ultimate Band List	http://american.recordings.com/wwwofmusic/ubl ubl.shtml	The Web's largest interactive list of music links.
Demographics		
Census Bureau	http://www.census.gov/	For U.S. demographic information
WWW Virtual Library Demography Studies	http://combs.anu.edu.au/ResFacilities/ DemographyPage.html	Hotlink into demographic studies on the Web
Statistical Resources on the Web	http://www.lib.umich.edu/libhome/Documents. center/stats.html	Stats including demographics, economics, health, education, etc.
Economics, etc.		
Antitrust Policy	http://www.vanderbilt.edu/Owen/froeb/ antitrust/antitrust.html	The latest news, case studies and research
Cliometric Society	gopher://cs.muohio.edu:70/11/library/govdocs	Archives specializing in economic history
China Home Page	http://utkvx1.utk.edu/~xurs/china.htm	Scientific, educational, business, and tourism information
Economic Report of the President	gopher://umslvma.umsl.edu:70/11/library /govdocs	Bill's view of the Economy

Economist Jokes	http://www.etla.fi/pkm/joke.html	How many economists does it take to screw in a light bulb?
I'm Europe	http://www.echo.lu/	European Economic Community programs and activities
Internet Guide to Japan Information Services	http://fuji.stanford.edu/XGUIDE	Business, legal, history, culture, travel, and much more.
Internet Marketing Archives	http://galaxy.einet.net:80/hypermail/inet-marketing	Access discussion groups related to marketing on the Internet.
Japanese Information	http://www.ntt.jp/japan/index.html	Traveling or moving to Japan? Valuable cultural/geographic information
Regional Economic Information System	http://govinfo.kerr.orst.edu/reis-stateis.html	Source for regional, state, and local data
World Factbook 1995	http://www.odci.gov/cia/publications/95fact/index.html	Detailed fact sheets on countries throughout the world
WWW Servers In Hong Kong	http://www.mit.edu:8001/ats/athena/user/s/y/syc/www/hkwww.html	Hotlink to a host of on-line sources in Hong Kong

For Fun and Profit

A Day in the Life Of Cyberspace	http://www.1010.org/	MIT Media Laboratory's Web site gives insight into the cutting edge In Cyberspace
Levi Strauss & Co.	http://www.levi.com/menu	One of the best commercial sites on the Web. Don't miss Fly Zone and Street with news from the streets of New York to Durban.
The Peeping Tom	http://www.ts.umu.se/~spaceman/camera.html	Take a PG-rated peek at the world from live shots of Manhattan to photos of Maui, and much more.
Security First National Bank	http://www.sfnb.com/	The first completely on-line bank.
Spiegels	http://www.spiegel.com/spiegel	Visit Spiegel's catalogs, magazine, and Loose Lips pages.
SportsZone	http://ESPNet.SportsZone.com/mlb/	Want more than box scores? Columns, team schedules, starting lineups. Like being there for the toss.
"The Spot"	http://www.thespot.com	The popular Generation X Cyberspace soap opera.
Toys R Us	http://www.tru.com/cgi-bin/coins/_810710984-17901_/toyshome.html	Toys R Us best sellers, directory of stores, and much more.
Toy Story	http://www.toystory.com~html	Toy Story: The Web Site. Meet the characters.
URouLette	http://www.uroulette.com:8000/	Take a spin on the Web. Who knows where you'll land?
Ziff Davis	http://www.ziff.com/	A tour of the Ziff empire.
Zima	http://www/wprd/com/servin2/index.html	Zima sponsored pages to the hip and happening.

(Continued)

Welcome to the Information Superhighway!

Information Please

AT&T Toll Free 800 Directory	http://www.tollfree.att.net/dir800/	Stop here to find any toll-free number.
Bartlett's Quotations	http://www.columbia.edu/acis/bartleby/bartlett	Find just the right quote here.
FedEx	http://www.fedex/com/SUCS_online.html	Track your package instantly.
Internet Resources	http://www.eit.com/web/netservices.html	A guide to information services on the Internet
Lexis-Nexis	http://www.meaddata.com	The commercial site for legal and business information services.
Library Information Servers	http://www.lib.washington.edu/~tdowling/libweb.html	A hotlink to libraries on the Internet
News Link	http://www.newslink.org	A hotlink to hundreds of newspapers, magazines and TV stations.
The Omnivore	http://history.cc.ukans.edu/carrie/news_main.html	World wide news from the perspective of the country of origin.
Pathfinder	http://www.pathfinder.com/	Connect to Time Warner publications.
Who's Who on Internet	http://web.city.ac.uk/citylive/pages.html	A compilation of non-commercial home pages on the Web.
The Virtual Reference Desk	http://frank.ntsu.edu/~kmiddlet/toddhome/uref.html	A hotlink for information from zip codes and census data to movie news.

266

About the Author

Kathy C. Yohalem is president and founder of Yohalem Ltd., a global strategic marketing company specializing in multimedia, communications, consumer products, manufacturing, retailing, fashion-related companies, and professional service firms.

Ms. Yohalem is a world-noted strategist and conceptualist with over 20 years experience in strategic marketing, planning, and new business development. She is an acknowledged authority on marketing strategy and electronic commerce, including strategic planning for clients in the new and changing channels involving on-line, the Web, CD-ROM, digital technology, and other new avenues of electronic distribution. She has also produced, hosted and merchandised home shopping shows.

As president of Yohalem Ltd., Ms. Yohalem's clients included Sears & Roebuck, Hanes, Sara Lee, Edgell Communications, and Dockers, among many others. Prior to running her own company, she held executive management positions with leading companies in the consumer products, manufacturing, retailing, and fashion-related industries including Garanimals, where she was responsible for the conceptualization and startup of the juvenile divisions. She is currently CEO of C-Source Communications LLC, a Coopers & Lybrand company. She also serves as director of strategic marketing and new business development with Coopers & Lybrand, LLP.

Ms. Yohalem lectures and speaks frequently at major industry conferences and seminars including The Wharton

School of Business, the National Sporting Goods Associa-
tion, the U.S. Department of Commerce, The Fragrance
Foundation, The National Retail Federation, the American
Apparel Manufacturers Association, and the American Bar
Association.

Ms. Yohalem has served as a columnist and contributing
editor to various trade and business publications and is frequently quoted in articles in prominent newspapers and
magazines.

Index

Dear Ms. Yohalem,

Please contact me to schedule a **free** consultation. I understand that a consultation does not obligate me in any way.

Name: _____ Title: _____
Business Name: _____
Address: _____
City: _____ State: _____ Zip: _____
Telephone: _____ Fax: _____ E-Mail Address: _____
No. Employees: _____ Annual Revenues: _____
No. Years in Business: _____

Describe your industry and the types of products or services you offer: _____
_____

_____

I want to learn more about:
❑ Strategic Marketing ❑ Brand Extension ❑ Globalization
❑ Licensing ❑ Electronic Commerce
❑ The Internet/Web Development ❑ CD-ROM ❑ Multimedia
❑ New Product/Service Development ❑ New Consumerism
❑ New Marketing Channels ❑ The Virtual Office
❑ Other _____
❑ I am interested in Think Tank Facilitation Services

Fax this completed form to 1-212-260-KCY1 (5291)
Call 212-473-6579
E-mail: kcyltd@inch.com
Or visit my **Web Site** at http://www.kcyltd.com/